Working with Disaffected Students

Contents

The authors

Professor Kathryn Riley, an international education consultant and Visiting Professor at The Institute of Education, London, led the World Bank's Effective Schools and Teachers Thematic Group from 1999-2001. Kathryn has been in education for many years, beginning as a volunteer teacher in Asmara Teacher Training Institute, Eritrea and then teaching in inner city schools in London, before holding senior academic positions at the University of Birmingham (at the Institute of Local Government Studies) and the University of Surrey Roehampton (where she was Director of the Centre for Educational Management). She has also been an elected councillor and senior officer in local government. She is particularly interested in how educational change takes place and the ways in which parents, communities, teachers and pupils can be brought into the change process. Current projects include, 'What Does it Take to be a Teacher in the 21st century?' Her publications are extensive and include the acclaimed, 'Whose School is it Anyway?' (Falmer Press, 1998); an extensive international reader, 'Leadership for Change and School Reform' (with Karen Seashore, Routledge Falmer, 2000); 'Leadership, learning and systemic reform' (Journal of Education Change, Volume 1).

Ellalinda Rustique-Forrester, was the lead research officer at the Centre for Educational Management on the project, 'Bringing Young People Back into the Frame'. Before coming to the UK, she taught in schools in New York City and was research associate for the US National Commission for Teaching and America's Future, at Teachers College, Columbia University, New York. She has particular expertise in teacher policy has recently completed an extensive review for the Institute of Public Policy Research on Teacher Supply, Learning from the USA.

Professor Mary Fuller, Department of Professional Education, Cheltenham and Gloucester College of Higher Education has been involved in research in schools and with adolescents since 1968. The span of her work has been considerable and includes pioneering work on race, gender and class issues in schools and on school culture. Mary has particular expertise in the field of continuing professional development of teachers.

David Rowles has a wide experience in education as a teacher of many years standing, Senior Inspector for Schools in the London Borough of Merton and Deputy Director of the Centre for Educational Management (where he was a Principal Researcher). His main areas of work have been on the implications of Ofsted inspections, the role of school governors and LEA reviews. David has considerable expertise in training, consultancy and evaluation.

Ron Letch started his career as a teacher in Essex. He then moved into teacher training as a senior lecturer in Education in Whitelands College. He went on to become a senior inspector for Surrey County and then chief inspector in the London Borough of Hounslow where he eventually became Deputy Director of Education for Hounslow. He was a Research Associate with the Centre for Educational Management where he led a number of projects.

Dr James Docking was Senior Research Officer at the Centre for Educational Management. He was formerly Head of the Education Department at Whitelands College and Chairman of the School of Education. Jim has published widely on managing behaviour in school, alienation in school, schools and parents, exclusion from school, special educational needs policy, and national education policy. In 2000 he edited New Labour's Policies for Schools: Raising the Standards (David Fulton).

Preface and acknowledgements

This book is about pupil disaffection. It tackles some of the thorny issues which policy-makers and practitioners are grappling with in many countries and contexts. Over recent years, education has become a political priority for many governments. Governments of different persuasions, including the UK government, have sought to deal with the issues of underachievement and failure. But if education is a political priority, why aren't school days 'the best days of your life'? Why are so many students – and their teachers – unhappy with their lot?

Fig. 1. I'm sad

By and large, most children start school at five, or thereabouts, with enthusiasm and curiosity. By and large, most parents want the best for their children. By and large, most teachers enter the teaching profession because they are motivated by enthusiasm for their subject, or by a commitment to support children's learning. By and large, those teachers who take the route to headship do so, not for the easy life, but because they want to make a difference to young people's lives. For many teachers and their pupils, education is a rewarding experience. But what happens over the years to lead to disaffection in a sizeable minority? Why does the partnership between schools and families succeed for some, but fall apart for others? Why do some young people reject school and become excluded from learning? What forces the different 'camps' into blame mode?

> Teacher/headteachers: *If only s/he (the recalcitrant pupil) would come to school more regularly.*
> Parents: *If only the teachers would listen.*
> Pupils: *If only the lessons weren't so boring.*

International studies have demonstrated that education attainment at 16 is the most important predictor of future participation in learning, and of labour-market opportunities. Young people with no qualifications are between two and three times more likely to be unemployed as their peers, and to be excluded from society. They become disenfranchised by their lack of educational opportunities.

This book is more than another tale of pupil disengagement. By talking to parents, pupils and teachers we have some answers to the questions:

- What can be done to realize the high expectations which are shared by parents, pupils and teachers alike when children first embark on the early years of their schooling?
- What can be done to make a difference?

Many adults and young people contributed their time, energy and thought to the challenging issues which are at the heart of this book. The book is based on an extended study of student disaffection carried out as a partnership between the authors, Lancashire County Council and Lancashire's two Training and Enterprise Councils. We have learned much through undertaking our work in Lancashire and I would like to thank all concerned for their contributions to the project. From the research team's point of view, the study has been a team effort but I would particularly like to thank Elle Rustique-Forrester for her contribution as lead researcher, Mary Fuller for helping set the project in train, Ian Monk and Belinda Stott for their enthusiastic back-up and David Rowles, Ron Letch and Jim Docking for their contributions to the fieldwork and analysis. Most of all, I would like to thank the young people we worked with, their parents and teachers.

This book is not about blame and punishment, but about analysis and solutions. I hope that the findings will contribute to making schools happier and more productive places to be – for teachers and pupils alike.

Kathryn A. Riley, May 2002

Foreword

The Inclusion Agenda brings with it challenges that have lain undisturbed for years in the education system. At one level, inclusion is a political issue. Governments see it from several angles: social justice for the individual, making education accessible and also a successful experience for all (the Standards Agenda), as well as part of a push to reduce crime and criminal behaviour. If education is to be an accessible and meaningful experience for every child, we need to create a 'Joined Up Agenda' (nationally and locally), and find individual solutions to individuals' problems.

Teachers and their unions have taken a variety of stances on inclusion which can be summed up as seeing the issue on at least two levels. The first is a professional response to the 'Inclusion Curriculum' and to the rights of all children, bearing in mind the interaction between the two, and the varying ways in which those issues play out in the different school contexts in which teachers find themselves. The second is a proper desire on the part of the teacher unions to see the health and safety of their members as paramount.

In thinking through the issues and our response to UK government policies over recent years, we came to realize in Lancashire that the factors which 'disenfranchise' a significant number of young people are complex and intricate, and that the national debate has tended to focus on the spectacular and obvious groups (disruptive, violent, etc.), although these tend to be the minority. In Lancashire, we wanted to find new ways of improving the prospects for young people by looking behind the headlines and finding out about the experience of children's disaffection from school from a range of vantage points.

The genesis of the project which is reported in this book came from discussions (between Kathryn Riley and her colleagues and myself) which stemmed from mutual concerns about the ways in which the issues surrounding disaffection were being thought about and acted on. Our discussions extended to wider debate with partners in Lancashire – local education authority colleagues, schools, Social Services and the Training and Enterprise Councils. We concluded that Kathryn and her team should be asked to construct a research and development project which would look at the stories of the disenfranchised, their parents and their teachers, in order to gain those crucial social and professional insights missing from the current debate.

For my part, the missing link is how to stimulate professional discussion and personal support for teachers and families in such a way as to enable all to succeed in a meaningful way, across a wide range of social and economic backgrounds in a large shire authority. The project has made a significant contribution to our thinking in Lancashire and forms a core part of our continuing debate. In looking at how children become frozen out of education, we are beginning to challenge current thinking on the causes of social exclusion, understand the complexities and build on successful practice.

This book is challenging, lively and informative. Its arguments and analysis are based on valid evidence and proper professional and academic constructs. It provides pointers to best practice which will be invaluable to policy-makers and practitioners alike, helping them to formulate and implement policies and practices which will support schools' efforts to improve the prospects for disaffected pupils. Committed teachers and educators will relish the professional challenges it offers. Every staff room should have its own copy of this book which should also be prescribed reading for Education Ministers.

Chris Trinick
Chief Executive, Lancashire County Council
June 2002

Part I
Introduction

1

School lives: fact and fiction

Fiction is littered with pupils' accounts of their schooldays and broadly speaking, there are three versions of events. Version one is about adventure and challenge – the plucky schoolgirls of Angela Brazil or the Chalet School, the aspiring wizards of Harry Potter. Version two is about rebellion – a disgruntled teenager's fantasy turns into macabre reality in the film *If*. Version three is about surviving adversity – enduring the bullying of other pupils (vividly described in *Tom Brown's School Days*), or the oppressive behaviour of teachers (Wackford Squeers in *Nicholas Nickleby*). More recent accounts of schooling (such as Ronald Searle's *Down with Skool*) dwell on the boredom and frustration.

When we think about children's experience of school, myth and reality, fact and fiction are closely intertwined. Adventure, challenge, rebellion, surviving adversity, boredom, bullying – school can be about any or all of these. Children, even in the same school, can experience school life in radically different ways. Much depends on what they bring to the school situation, as well as the ways in which the school interprets that experience. Jane Eyre's bitter immersion into school life at Lowood was exacerbated by the dire warning given about her (by Mr Brocklehurst, manager of the Institution) to teachers and pupils alike, 'Children, you must be on your guard against her ... shun her example, if necessary avoid her company ... Teachers, you must watch her, keep your eyes on her movements ... This girl ...this child is a liar' (Brontë, 1980, p. 87). But surely today, schools could not be so ruthless? .... Could they?

This book tells a complex story. One side of the story is about frustration, sadness, disappointment and anger. No parent or educator can be unmoved by the accounts of rejection which are described in Chapter 4. We recognize, too, that our story is a partial one. In focusing on children on the margins – those who for whatever reason are rejected by school or who feel rejected by it – we have drawn attention to the unhappy and failing, not to the happy and successful. In highlighting the experiences of the disaffected, we are looking at the minority and not the majority because our story is about them. We know that schools do many good things, for many children and young people. We do not want to mask those achievements but what we do want to do is to draw attention to the ways in which schools can be healthier and more productive places for all pupils – and their teachers.

Our story is also a profoundly optimistic one. When you read it, we hope that you will see two things: first, the commitment of so many teachers and education professionals – the ideas, the creative energy, the many successes in dealing with pupil disaffection. Secondly, the ways in which an education community which is open about its problems and failures, as well as its ambitions and aspirations can through listening to the disparate voices – particularly those of disengaged young people and their parents – find new ways of creating success for its young people.

As Chris Trinick has said in his Foreword, the issues of disaffection are complex and the extremes only too familiar to us through press reports or professional grapevines: the pupil who vandalizes the school, the parent who abuses teachers. There is also the other side of the disaffection coin: the teacher who strikes a child, the headteacher who ignores bullying with dire consequences. Whatever the story, it is more likely to be about blame than about explanation or resolution.

This book is not about apportioning blame – pupils, parents, teachers or society. We start with the basic premise that those children and young people who did not have a challenging and fulfilling education are in effect *disenfranchised* from society, socially and economically. This premise is based on fundamental notions about social justice and entitlement to learning in what is frequently described these days, as the 'knowledge society'.

It may seem strange to talk about entitlement to learning in a UK national context in which all children have the right to attend school, without cost, throughout their statutory years of schooling. Formally, those opportunities do exist. However, many children and young people become disadvantaged by the *process* of schooling: the cumulative impact of the demands on teachers, the competitive pressures generated by national demands, as well as by the varying needs of students themselves. Many current policy solutions are still dependent on deficit models which blame the learner for not taking the opportunities which are available to them, without acknowledging the ways in which educational processes can exclude individuals, or groups. Not enough attention is given to the voices of learners themselves, or to the ways in which changes in practice are needed to encourage people to return to learning, and to maximize learning opportunities.

This book is about how to widen and expand education opportunities to a marginalized group of young people – awkward, difficult and challenging though they might be. We do not underestimate the difficulties. We know from our own professional experiences as teachers, as well as through this project, the ways in which disengaged and disaffected students can disrupt an otherwise enthusiastic class of learners, or generate exhaustion, even amongst the most committed and skilled teachers. But we also have come to see the ways in which this might change.

We began the work which is described in this book as a study on disaffection: a search for the policies and practices which could provide the basis for a successful policy on social inclusion. Over a period of some two years, we explored a range of issues surrounding student disaffection, including those with which many teachers grapple on a daily basis. In every stage of our work, we have tried to look at events and challenges in the round – what happened, and why, from the different vantage points of all concerned. Through a creative partnership with administrators, teachers, and local politicians in Lancashire, as well as through the openness of pupils and parents, we were able to question and challenge and to gain important insights.

Through the course of our work, we have come to understand much about the boundaries within which teachers and headteachers operate, and the ways in which they are sometimes constrained from being the educators they might wish to be. We have also learned much about the ways in which children and young people start on the downward spiral of misbehaviour and low expectations, and become locked into a pattern of behaviour from which they find it hard to break free.

We started by looking at the nature of the problem. Who are the disaffected? What are the factors which seem to contribute to their exclusion from education, from unemployment and ultimately, from society? We came to see that the group of disaffected young people is wide-ranging and is connected to issues of gender, race and ethnic origin and class. It includes the rootless young men who no longer see themselves as having access to the skilled and unskilled manual occupations of the past, as well as the young women who disappear into early maternity – with consequences for themselves and their children. It includes the truants, the drop-outs, those who are formally excluded from school, the disillusioned and the disengaged, and all those for whom schooling is a disappointing and unhappy experience (see Box 1.1).

Box 1.1 Starting points

- Educational attainment at 16 is the most important predictor of future participation in learning and of labour market opportunities. Young people with no qualifications are between two and three times more likely to be unemployed as their peers, and to be excluded from society.
- Young people are disenfranchised when they are formally excluded from school, when they truant, when they leave school with no examinations and when they are disengaged from learning.
- No matter who is to 'blame', those children and young people who do not receive a challenging and fulfilling education are, in effect, socially and economically *disenfranchised* from society.

We have learned many lessons from carrying out our work and will emphasize three at this point. *The first is that the key to change lies in rethinking the nature of teaching and learning.* Whilst there are many good projects and initiatives which 'deal' with student disaffection, more weight needs to be given to recognizing the diverse ways in which children learn, as well as the fragmented nature of schooling for so many.

A second key lesson (which has struck us time and time again during the course of our explorations) *is that you cannot underestimate the importance of the interplay between teachers and pupils.* Vulnerable students attach great weight to their relationships with their teachers. If children feel that they are neither liked nor respected, they find it particularly difficult to learn. Place a vulnerable child in the orbit of a disaffected teacher, and the outcomes are predictable and grim.

A third key lesson is that the solutions to the problems which are described in this book, and which will be familiar to many of you, lie within the grasp of those involved in them. So often during the course of the study, we have thought ourselves to be an 'Education Relate' service, the counsellor, the go-between who brings together the warring factions, the individuals and groups in dispute with each other and say, 'whilst you may have different views about who is to blame, you are all agreed about what needs to be done'. Ultimately, this book is about what can be done, and how. We offer what, we hope, is a fresh approach to thinking about student disaffection, and ideas about policy and practice which will be of benefit to practitioners and policy-makers alike.

The book is divided into four parts. Part I is the introduction and Part II is very much scene setting. We review the national and international context, highlighting the ways in which these influence our thinking about inclusion. We also examine the extent of exclusion in England, and the factors and assumptions which shape current policies and practices. For those readers with a particular research interest, we also explain briefly how we went about our study. In Part III, we look at disaffection from the vantage point of the different 'experts' – disaffected children and their parents, teachers and headteachers. How does each group perceive the issues and challenges? What practices and approaches appear to be working, and why? Finally, in Part IV, by bringing together what first appear to be disparate voices, we look at what can be done to create the foundations for a policy on inclusion – what can be done to make a difference. The ideas that we put forward come from pupils, parents, teachers and other educators. We offer practical illustrations which we feel will be helpful to policy-makers, schools and practitioners alike, not just in the UK but elsewhere.

Part 2
Setting the Scene

2

A problem shared?

The nature and extent of exclusion

Many industrialized countries are witnessing growing levels of social exclusion and, what many politicians deem to be, unacceptably high levels of failure, drop-out and truancy. According to international data, low levels of educational attainment are common in between 15 and 30 per cent of school-age children. Underperforming students include many who have the capacity to achieve and fulfil a national curriculum (OECD, 1996a). Student performance varies by country, gender and location but, regardless of the source of difficulties experienced at school, there are large differences between the attainment levels of the weakest 25 per cent of pupils and the strongest. Generally, this difference is the equivalent of two years but it can amount to as much as five years (OECD, 1997).

Government views about the causes of underperformance and exclusion, and about the remedies vary. Notions of failure and exclusion are culturally specific. Young people in Denmark or Sweden, for example, cannot be formally excluded from a school, as they can be in the UK or the USA (Osler and Hill, 1998; Parsons, 1999). Carl Parsons, a leading researcher in the field, has drawn attention to the disparities in exclusion rates between countries, describing the UK policy climate as one in which 'unprecedented numbers of children are being excluded from school – the rate being far in excess of that in any other western European country' (Parsons, 1999, p. 1). Definitions of 'school failure' also vary across different cultures. For many countries, the English concept of a 'failing' school (i.e. one that has failed to meet national inspection standards, as judged by the Office for Standards in Education, OFSTED) is an alien one.

Although cultural differences about the *definitions and processes* of school failure differ, the *indicators of what count as failure* are widely shared. Common indicators that schools are failing to meet students' academic needs include: low or below-average test scores; a high incidence of school exclusion or expulsion; low attendance or high drop-out rates; and low percentages of students taking national examinations or continuing in further education.

National concerns about failure and underachievement are shaped by global factors, such as, increasing economic competitiveness, the move towards a knowledge-based society. National performance matters, particularly in relation to that of your economic competitor – hence the continued attention which governments pay to their performance on international league tables, such as The International Mathematics and Science Study (TIMSS) now in its third incarnation.[1] Politicians have come to realize that economic prosperity is dependent on the creation of a workforce which is able to manipulate knowledge, information and ideas. Countries and regions which are not part of the knowledge and information revolution will be left behind (OECD, 1995; Riley 1998a; 1998b). Equally, those citizens who are excluded from the foundations of learning will also become excluded from society, subject not only to higher levels of unemployment and poverty than their peers, but also poorer health. International data has also highlighted the growing inequalities of income and personal resources in many Organization for Economic Co-operation and Development (OECD) countries (OECD, 1995), generating concerns about social cohesion, either as a matter of social justice, or as a factor which might lead to the emergence of an underclass which could rock the foundations of society (see Box 2.1).

Two indicators of exclusion are absence rates (an indication of truancy) and formal exclusions from school. Absence rates – calculated as the percentage of half days missed as a result of staying away from school without permission – have remained unchanged in England since 1994, at 0.7 per cent (DfEE, 2000a). Formal exclusion rates have changed over time. In 1990/91, the number of pupils excluded from schools in England stood at around 3,000. By 1996/97, this figure had escalated to 12,700 (DfEE, 1999), but by 1997/98 it had fallen back by 3 per cent (to 12,300), and by 1998/99 by a further 15 per cent (to 10,400). Thirteen per cent of the children excluded from school are from primary schools, 83 per cent

Box 2.1 A problem shared?
- Failure and exclusion are culturally specific. (In some countries, young people cannot be formally excluded from a school, in others, the notion of a 'failing' school is an alien one.)
- Common indicators of failure are low or below-average test scores; a high incidence of school exclusion or expulsion; low attendance or high drop-out rates; and low percentages of students taking national examinations or continuing in further education.
- Politicians have seen exclusion as a national priority because of global competition, the move towards a knowledge-based society and fears about the creation of an isolated underclass.

from secondary and 4 per cent from special schools (DfEE, 2000a).

Particular groups of pupils appear to be vulnerable to exclusion. Eight out of ten excluded pupils are male (ibid.) and one in four are, or have been, in the care of a local authority (Castle and Parsons, 1997). A disproportionately high number of excluded pupils are from black and ethnic minority communities and recent studies have shown that black pupils are up to six times more likely to be excluded than white (Osler and Hill, 1998).[2] In 1998, in an attempt to reduce exclusions, the UK government set targets to reduce truancy and permanent exclusions by a third by the year 2002 (SEU, 1998).

The education agenda

In 1997, an incoming Labour government made education a top political priority in the UK. 'Education, Education, Education' became the now familiar personal mantra of Prime Minister Tony Blair. At the top of the agenda was the issue of school standards and performance. The new Labour government set national targets for improving student performance; reinforced the inspection framework for schools (which had been introduced by the previous Conservative administration); required local education authorities (LEAs) to demonstrate how, through their Education Development Plans (EDPs), they could ensure that school improvement took place (School Standards and Framework Act, 1998); and introduced a plethora of funding initiatives (such as Education Action Zones) aimed at raising performance.[3,4]

Issues about school exclusions were part of a linked agenda on social disaffection which was supported by the establishment of various national committees and a specialized national governmental unit. A range of initiatives aimed at tackling social disadvantage were introduced, such as the 'New Deal' which placed an emphasis on positive training and employment outcomes for marginalized young people.[5]

In a parallel study to our work in Lancashire, one of our team members carried out an extensive review of the range of UK national initiatives on social exclusion. This work revealed competing demands, expectations and assumptions (Riley and Skelcher, 1998), as well as weak connections between differing initiatives at both national and local levels (Riley and Watling, 1999). Whilst attempts were made at a national level to create greater synergy between different initiatives, our experience suggested that this had yet to filter through to the world of practice.[6] We concluded that national imperatives, including funding priorities, had tended to favour approaches which reacted to the 'problem' of student disaffection, rather than those which sought to avert problems at an early stage. The complexities of different funding regimes and the speed at which many national initiatives had been introduced by a range of government departments and agencies (each with their own perspectives and priorities) had added to the problems (Riley and Skelcher, 1998).

The UK's dual policy focus on standards and inclusion created both new opportunities and resource possibilities, whilst also generating tensions. Professionals working in the broad field of school and student support found themselves faced with a plethora of initiatives (from government and external sources) which ranged from training for employability, to reducing youth offending. At a school level, many teachers felt caught out by the government's twin track agenda, perhaps seeing the government as 'Janus', the god who faces two ways, in this case asking them to reconcile what often appeared to be conflicting agendas: standards and inclusion. When the accountability stakes are high and schools are judged in terms of their examination performance and success in OFSTED inspections, broader social or educational goals tend to be put on the back burner, and children on the margins seen as obstacles to the achievement of national goals.[7]

Educational achievement matters

Research studies have shown consistently that educational attainment at age 16 is the most important predictor of future participation in learning, and of labour-market prospects. The skills, knowledge and qualifications acquired by individuals will, to a large degree, determine their participation in society (Pearce and Hillman, 1998). Exclusion from learning has many consequences, not only for excluded individuals, but also for society as a whole.

In the UK, students are 'excluded' from schooling in a number of ways, and for a number of reasons. There is the group we have already talked about, those who are formally excluded from school, sometimes because the head and governors have difficulty finding alternatives for pupils whose chronic absence, truancy and behaviour present the school with a challenging management problem. Many have argued that the climate of growing competition between schools, coupled with the national inspection system and the publication of league tables of school performance, appear to have contributed to a rise in pupil exclusions (see Box 2.2).

Those children who are formally excluded from school are the most visible part of the problem, but whilst formal exclusion is a critical issue,

---

Box 2.2 Some views about the rise in student disaffection

A number of researchers studying social exclusion and other related aspects of school disaffection, such as pupil absenteeism and truancy (Hoyle, 1998), emotional and behaviour difficulties (Cooper et al., 1993), and school discipline and misbehaviour (Lovey et al., 1993; Docking, 1996; Lovey 2000), have suggested that recent political reforms in the UK may have contributed to the relatively high levels of social and school disaffection. Contributing factors are often said to be greater competition between schools through school choice and market-driven polices (Riley, 1998a; Whitty et al., 1998), increased school and teacher accountability through national league tables and school inspection (Robinson, 1998; Whitty et al., 1998) and reinforced standardization of curriculum and pedagogy through national assessments, examinations and the curriculum (Lovey et al., 1993; McEwan and Thompson, 1997).

it is a symptom of a more complex and profound set of problems. The second and equally worrying 'excluded' group comprises those young people who leave schools with no examinations. In the UK, this represents some 8 per cent of young people (House of Commons, 1998). In some of the most difficult and deprived areas in the USA, as few as 1 in 16 students graduate from high school (Kozol, 1996). As we said in the introductory chapter, international data indicates that young people without upper secondary qualifications are between three and five times more likely to become unemployed than their peers (OECD, 1996b). Those who leave school before the standard 'graduation' date in their country are at particular risk of unemployment and long-term social exclusion (OECD, 1996c). Many of this group will be male, but there is also a vulnerable group of young women who disappear into early maternity and find themselves on the margins of society, with consequences not only for themselves but also for their children.

A third group of young people are those who attend school for at least some of the time, but are disengaged or marginalized by their school experience – silent participants who are made invisible by their school life. The behaviour of these students is characterized by inconsistent attendance and work habits, and non-participation in lessons or homework assignments. Many will eventually exercise the 'exit' option, to the relief of stressed teachers, and remove themselves physically from school, by truanting or dropping out. Some of this group will have learning difficulties but others may be children of marked ability who – if their needs are not met – become difficult and who 'self-select' out of education, although they usually manage to avoid formal exclusion. Some will be excluded by lack of access to technology in their own homes, although this is an issue which is beginning to be tackled. Whoever these young people are, there is growing evidence to suggest that negative experiences of school carry through into adulthood, influencing views about future learning and attitudes about school which may then be passed on to the next generation.

This critical issue was brought sharply into focus in a Swedish study which traced the school careers of some 1,200 young people, questioning them at the ages of 13 and 18, and then in a second study, at the age of 21, three years after they had left school (Bengt-Andersson, 1997;

Lindblad, 1997). The study showed that for about a third of all students, school had been a positive, meaningful and stimulating experience. The students felt that they had had good contacts with their teachers and had been involved in the life of the school. A second group, again about a third, appeared to have tolerated school, although they were discontented with many aspects of their school life. For the third group, school was a profoundly disappointing and largely unhappy experience which offered them little creative or intellectual stimulation.

A particularly disturbing finding from the Swedish study was that students' perceptions of their school situation at age 18 had changed little by the time they were 21. If young people perceive school as a negative experience when they are pupils, this perception tends to be carried through into adulthood, influencing views about future learning and, possibly, attitudes about school which are then passed on to the next generation. The consequences of an unhappy school experience can be far-reaching, not only for the individual experiencing it.

As part of our preparation for the project, we carried out a review of the current body of research on disaffection and exclusion.[8,9] Our observations from the review are that the debate on social exclusion has not paid sufficient attention to *how* schools and teachers might rethink and devise more inclusive policies and practices for teaching and learning. The continuing emphasis on the conditions of social disadvantage, and on social intervention strategies based on notions of pupils' deficits, has drawn attention away from any systematic exploration of innovative and school-based solutions. This book is about looking at some of those solutions.

3

Putting the study in place

In this chapter we continue our scene setting by describing how we went about our study. This is not compulsory reading. If this is not your interest, you might want to move straight on to Chapter 4 to find out what the young people in our study thought. You can always come back to this section at a later stage, but if you are interested in the background, then read on.

The specific local context for our study was Lancashire, a region in north-west England which supports over 600 schools, plus a range of education and training initiatives. Lancashire is a large county which serves a socially and ethnically diverse population located in rural areas, as well as in a number of towns. Within the county, there are significant pockets of high unemployment and social disadvantage, and high proportions of pupils from these areas are considered disenfranchised.

Our work took place in Lancashire for a number of reasons. First, Lancashire had already collaborated with us in a major project on the role and effectiveness of local education authorities.[1] Through this project we had developed good working relationships with various agencies within Lancashire, and gained an understanding of the issues and challenges which faced the locality. More importantly, we had (as Chris Trinick explained in his Foreword) come to share some common concerns about pupil disaffection. Those concerns ultimately became the basis for our study and helped shape the project partnership between ourselves – (as the research and development team) the Lancashire County Council (parents, teachers and other educators, and of course pupils) and the two local Training and Enterprise Councils.[2]

We had three questions in mind when we began our work:

- Who are the disenfranchised?
- What are the factors that contribute to their exclusion from education, employment and ultimately from society?
- And (perhaps more importantly) what strategies and approaches are most likely to succeed in tackling these problems?

In trying to answer those questions, we designed the project to enable us to capture the views and experiences of a number of 'excluded' young people and their parents, and to be able to contrast those views with the perceptions of the professionals who work with them (teachers, head-teachers, youth and community workers, pupil welfare staff), as well as the policy-makers and senior administrators who help shape the local climate.

We began our work in 1998. Our starting point was to try and identify the scale of disaffection in the county. We have already highlighted the main indicators of disaffection in the previous chapter: non-attendance rates (i.e. unauthorized absences), permanent exclusions and the percentage of pupils leaving with no examinations. Lancashire differed little from the national norm on the first two indicators, but had fewer students leaving without any examinations at all (see Table 3.1). These

Table 3.1 Profile of pupil disaffection (1997 – 98)

Indicators of school disaffection	Lancashire	National
Total number of schools:	502 Primary 89 Secondary 31 Special 30 Nursery	
% non-attendance * (unauthorized and authorized)*	6%	6.1%
Total number of permanent exclusions	335	12,298
(secondary and primary pupils)*	(.17)	(.16)
% of 15 year-olds leaving school with no qualifications (GCSE / GNVQ)**	4%	6%

Based on:
* 1997/98 data reported and published in Lancashire Behaviour Support Plan, 1999.
** GA1 1997/98 Examinations Results, Lancashire Educational Authority, 3 March 1999 Report.

indicators do not, of course, show all the young people who are at the margins of school life and who have, in effect, opted out of learning. However, they provided us with some sense of the scale of disaffection and enabled us to begin to think about the overlap, between the different categories of pupils, and between schools and support agencies.

We gave considerable thought to our research methods and decided to adopt a qualitative approach to our fieldwork that was highly developmental and interactive. This approach has yielded rich detail and enabled us to capture the diverse experiences and perceptions of a wide range of LEA officers, project co-ordinators, social workers, teachers, headteachers, school-based professionals, parents and pupils.[3] We carried out our work in linked phases and in Figure 3.1 illustrate the connections between those phases.

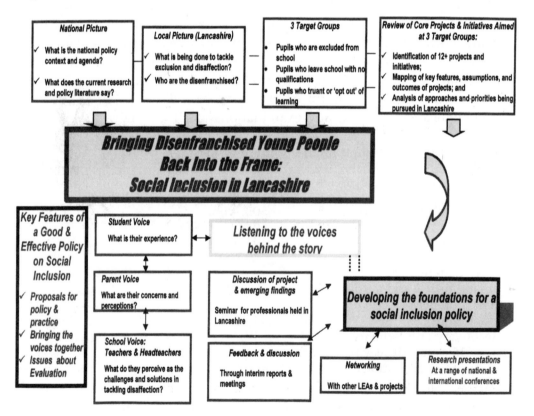

Fig. 3.1 Key elements of Riley/Rustique-Forrester the Lancashire Project

Having completed our mapping of the national, research and policy agendas, we undertook a systematic audit of a range of projects and initiatives in Lancashire aimed at tackling disaffection and promoting social inclusion. We identified 12 specific initiatives which represented a cross-section of those in operation and tried to draw out the lessons from these. At this stage, we focused on the voices of non-school-based professionals, listening to their views about the young people they were working with, as well as their experiences in developing projects and implementing initiatives and delivering specialist services.

As part of this process, we held a number of meetings with a wide range of professionals, to check our understandings with them about what we had found. We also held a seminar in which we presented a template which summarized the key features of the main projects on disaffection (the impetus for the project, the agency involvement, the target population, the project goals and outcomes, etc.). We have presented a modified version of this template in Chapter 10. Following this period of feedback and reflection, we completed a first project report which was discussed widely.[4]

Next, we turned our attention to some of the other voices. What did all of this look like from their vantage point? In this phase of our work we focused on pupils, parents and schools, teachers and headteachers.[5] Our aim was to examine how each group viewed the problem of disaffection; what they identified as the factors within school that either aggravated and reinforced problems or helped prevent and reduce disaffection; and what they believed to be the solutions. Were there particular approaches and practices that appeared to be working? The focus of exploration is described in more detail in Box 3.1.

Having listened to these different voices, we wrote a second project report which focused on the policy and practice issues and presented this in November 2000 to a conference for secondary headteachers. By the time we had completed our work in Lancashire, we had held formal meetings or conducted interviews with some 140 individuals, some on several occasions. We had also held more informal interactions with a further 240 other individuals forming a wider group, bringing the total number of people involved in the project to approximately 380.[6] In the next section, we begin to tell their story.

Box 3.1 Listening to the different voices

Pupil voice. At an early stage, we recognized that young people are an important 'expert' voice who can help schools and policy-makers identify those factors that can make a significant difference in improving the educational opportunities for young people. Working with colleagues in Lancashire we set up a number of student panels, aimed at hearing the voice of disengaged young people across the county. To create an environment in which the students would feel comfortable and also free to express their views, we held the panels in non-school settings. The panels included truanting, disaffected and excluded students. We tried to identify the problems which the young people were experiencing, as well as the strategies that appeared to be making a positive difference to their education experience.

Parent Voice. As parents are key partners in education, we tried to capture something of the views, interpretations and perceptions of a number of parents of disaffected pupils. We wanted to understand the school and non-school issues that, in their view, contributed to school disaffection, and to establish which projects or approaches were working for which young person and why. It was very difficult to reach parents and we were only able to do so through the support of the Education Welfare Service.

School voice (teachers and headteachers). The other key partners in the education process are, of course, teachers and headteachers. We anticipated that our work with them would shed light on the kinds of national and local policies needed to reduce student disengagement; the ways in which school policies and classroom practices might need to change; and the effectiveness or otherwise of the different local initiatives and approaches aimed at tackling exclusion and disaffection. This certainly proved to be the case. Our interviews with both groups also gave us some fresh insights into the ways in which external pressures (such as the need to achieve national performance targets) generate internal pressures within schools. It also helped us understand the growing and diverse demands on schools from pupils and parents today, as well as from governments.

Part 3
Telling Tales out of School

4

Children's voices

Perceptions and realities

A UK National Theatre Production *Life Times Three* (by Jasmina Reza) tells the story of two couples who spend a fraught evening together, instead of what was intended to be a pleasant social event. Each brings to that encounter their own emotional baggage, their own views of the other characters and their own realities. As the play unfolds, the story is told from the perspective of each of the different characters. Each retelling provides new images and insights, but also reveals contradictions and inconsistencies. By the end of the play we are left wondering – who is telling the truth?

In telling the stories of disenfranchised young people and the many others who have parts to play in their story, we did not seek to establish one truth, but to establish perceptions: what do all of those involved – in what are often difficult situations – think about events? We adopted this approach, not to try and reconcile the different versions of reality, but to see how and where misunderstandings arise and whether there are similar experiences, explanations and, even more crucially, common solutions.

Our first scene tells the story from the pupils' side. The young people we involved in our pupil panels were not a cross-section of the student population. They were included because they had already been identified as being disaffected or excluded. Running the panels was not an easy task. Even as ex-teachers with extensive teaching experience[1] we found the task a challenging one, and were grateful to our partners in Lancashire for their help. We were also reminded why, during our earlier classroom teaching days, we had so often felt exhausted on a Friday night. We learned much from listening to the painful and moving stories of those who see themselves as being at the bottom of the heap.

In carrying out the pupil panels we had three objectives:

- to gain a better understanding of the causes and dynamics of young people's disaffection and disengagement from school, and from the learning process;
- to identify the factors which they thought could make a positive difference in their schooling experience;
- to examine whether current efforts aimed at tackling disaffection and exclusion appeared to be having any positive impact on their experiences in schools, and in classrooms.

We told the 45 young people involved in our study that their views were important and that although our work was unlikely to help them personally, it would benefit other children and young people. They rose to that challenge. The five panels (of eight to ten students) each ran for a full day. We interviewed 25 girls and 20 boys between the ages of 11 and 16 and found it more difficult to get the boys to discuss the issues than the girls. We made it clear to the young people that, whilst we would ensure that they could not be personally identified by anything they said to us, we planned to feedback our overall findings to the county, schools and teachers, to help them make decisions about policy and practice. We asked them to be as thoughtful as possible about their experiences and difficulties in school and their opinions about what might need to change.

We used a variety of ways to find out what they thought, including small and large groups discussions and a card sort exercise (where the young people were asked to range items in order of importance). We also introduced a 30-minute drawing activity to provide a break in the day's discussion and to offer students another vehicle for expressing their feelings. For this activity, students were asked to draw a picture or construct a diagram (e.g. spider map) that showed what it felt like to be at school. The images drawn by the young people, and the words they used in relation to those images, displayed their anxieties, frustrations – and hopes. We have used a number of those illustrations throughout the book.

Learning was a fragmented, inconsistent and interrupted experience

Schools operate on the basis of a number of assumptions. One is that young people come to school on time, daily and with no interruptions to their learning. The reality, of course, is far removed from this. For many pupils, learning is a fragmented, inconsistent and interrupted experience. There are a range of reasons why this is the case, some to do with the absences and attitudes of students themselves. However, learning opportunities are also interrupted because of teachers' absences through illnesses, or because of the inability of the school to recruit specialist staff.

Some pupils in our study experienced a high turnover of teachers, repetition and gaps in the school's attempt to teach the curriculum. Many interpreted the failure of the school to find a suitable teacher replacement as a rejection of them. One group of young women were particularly aggrieved at the failure, as they saw it, of their school to find a replacement child development teacher. The lack of dialogue between the students as learners, and between those who were supposed to be supporting their learning, exacerbated this sense of rejection and reinforced pupils' view that they were at the bottom of the pile.

According to their account, students also missed out on learning opportunities because of school discipline policies. Some were put 'on ice' – in isolation, a room in which pupils were placed following a number of warnings about their behaviour (see Chapter 5). Children on 'ice' were separated from their peers, in their view outcasts from the daily life of the school, unable to move forward. 'You sit there and do nothing', '[Isolation] is a good place to go if you want to sleep', they told us. Others were sent to a behaviour unit which was described as a boring experience where you did no work and one which had limited impact on their behaviour: 'It didn't do nothing to change me' was a typical comment. The cycle of bad behaviour, rejection and physical isolation was difficult to break.

Fragmentation in the learning process also occurred because of absence from school. Many of our interviewees were 'in and out' of school for a variety of reasons – but whatever the reason, re-entry was a major stumbling block. Erratic attendance led to sarcastic comments from teachers such as, 'Oh you have finally decided to join us today then, have you?' One boy, returning after a long absence, was told that he 'should just go back home', which he did. Pupils described re-entry as a lonely and isolated business, and reintegration as difficult (see Fig. 4.1). One form teacher 'welcomed' back another student, a long-term truant, by encouraging the class to clap – slowly. Pupils felt there was little or no effort to help them make up for lost time, or to ensure that they had continuity of teaching. With only a few exceptions, schools did not appear to have policies in place to help pupils catch up on missing work, nor did form teachers appear to oversee whether young people were up to date with their work. The extent to which pupils were able to keep up with the flow of work depended, to a large degree, on the good will of their friends, from whom they copied notes. There are many reasons why schools are unable to maintain these connections, as we discuss later in the book.

Fig. 4.1   I don't belong

Relationships matter

Pupils' views about school were shaped by a number of key people and interactions. It was:

- an amalgam of the quality and consistency of their interactions with individual teachers;
- a set of encounters with the physical environment;
- a social network – a source of friendship and amusement, but also rejection.

Relationships with teachers were key. Many of the pupils we met were vulnerable for a number of reasons – including major pressures at home, as well as acute learning difficulties – and were susceptible to the highs and lows of school life. Their experience suggested that encounters with one or two hectoring teachers could tip the balance in their behaviour and send them spiralling down the path of exclusion, or truanting from school. Equally, too, the support and endorsement of key teachers who understood their needs could keep them on track.

Both female and male students could identify with teachers who were 'human', 'laughing', 'smiling', they 'made jokes' and were 'fair to everyone'. 'Good' teachers were those who 'explained things well' and demonstrated a sense of fairness, equity and humanity. They 'took the time to help' and 'treated you like a person', not 'like a baby'. 'Good' teachers were those who were able to make a connection between the classroom and the daily lives and experiences of young people. Students liked going to their classes ''cos you feel good', and because of that 'you actually learn something in their lessons'. 'Good' teachers were not 'just easy teachers ''cos', as one student explained, 'no one wouldn't respect them'. Students' perceptions of good and bad teachers are summarized in Table 4.1. Many of these perceptions about 'good' teachers are similar to those which have emerged in earlier research (e.g. Docking, 1987, pp. 71–9).

The other side of the coin were those teachers who shouted and talked at students, who failed to connect with them as individuals, and who were inconsistent in their attitudes and behaviour. We found that whilst most of the girls could identify with at least one teacher, who knew and understood them and was sympathetic and responsive, few of the boys could do so. Examples of bad teachers were legion. 'Bad' teachers were inconsistent, shrill and, in extreme cases, guilty of manhandling students, grabbing them by the neck, shoulder or arm. One female Year 7 student described how one teacher had poked her on the forehead and called her a 'stupid little pest'. Sarcasm and humiliation were used to maintain order and discipline.

Table 4.1 Students' perceptions of 'good' and 'bad' teachers

'Good' teachers were described as:	'Bad' teachers were seen as:
• Helpful and supportive • Taking the time to explain material in-depth	• Mean and unfair • Unwilling to help or explain material and ideas beyond instruction
• Friendly and personable	• Judgemental of pupils' parents and siblings
• Understanding and knowing subject well	• Routine and unchanging in their teaching styles and methods
• Using a variety of teaching styles and innovative approaches	• Inflexible and disrespectful of pupils
• Fair and having equal standards and expectations for pupils, regardless of their test scores	• Unaware of and unsympathetic to pupils' personal problems
• Willing to reward pupils for progress.	• Physically intimidating and verbally abusive.

Pupils offered a range of observations about teachers' behaviour, teaching styles and the levels of tolerance that different teachers had towards their pupils. Some teachers were seen as being 'too old', and younger teachers were often seen as being more understanding. According to the pupils, some teachers 'need to take courses to teach better'. Pupils were particularly critical of those teachers who were rigid, lacked understanding and were unfair, or were determined that 'everything must be right'.

Many pupils felt that they had been less fairly treated than some of their peers, and that teachers had lower expectation of them because they were seen as being less able. '[The teachers] should treat us like other ones – they treat them like gods – ''cos they do their work in a matter of seconds', explained one student. 'That is 'cos they're up to the standard they expect,' added another. Descriptions about teachers and their interactions with students also included unsettling suggestions from female and male students, in two different panels, that male teachers made female students feel uncomfortable, physically and verbally. Several students told of a male teacher who 'looks up girls' skirts as they walk upstairs'. In another panel, male and female students said that one teacher openly made fun of women and his wife in the classroom. 'I think he's sexist,' one female student stated.

Students also recognized the tremendous demands on teachers, and the ways in which their behaviour and that of other pupils contributed to the build-up of tensions in the classroom. One male student described the headteacher and teachers as 'rushing about looking stressed'. Many pupils described most of their teachers, as 'stressed out by teaching' and 'pressured', observing that perhaps teachers' jobs were 'not easy these days'. One pupil argued, 'I don't think that some teachers are prepared for teaching ... I don't think they knew how hard teaching us would be'.

They were labelled as failures

Many students expressed the view that once they, and other students, had got into a downward spiral of bad behaviour, exclusion and non-attendance, the chances of improving their prospects in the school were almost nil. In one panel, six out of ten students claimed that at some time they had been in at least one or two of the top ability sets, but that once they had 'fallen down, it was hard to get backup'. The common feeling across pupils from all the schools was that very little was expected from them. Students characteristically described their schools as 'not listening to us or what we would like'. A male student said, 'My school thinks I'm dumb'. Another boy, who had been in the top set for five subjects but whose poor behaviour had caused him to be demoted, said, 'I don't give

a f... now. They're not going to let me get any GCSEs so I just p... about.'
One girl said that in her school 'teachers don't give you a chance: my
sister had the whole of Year 10 off ... she's now back in Year 11 and they're
saying that she's only going to get Cs and Ds in her GCSEs'.

Other students claimed that they had been labelled as potential trouble-
makers on the basis of the track record of brothers and sisters or, in several
cases, because of the behaviour of their own parents as past pupils in the
school. One particular group of young women aged 15, were deeply
cynical and saw school as something that they were almost programmed
to dislike. One female student stated, 'My mum hated it and I am just
like her'. Another girl said rather emphatically, 'Teachers will never
change'. Yet another student (whose parents had previously attended his
school) said that a member of staff had told him, 'Your parents were no
good, and you're no good either'. In one panel, pupils claimed that
teachers often treated them as lost causes because of their reputation in
school and were happy for them to be isolated (either in school or sent
to 'isolation'), so that that rest of the class could get on with the lesson
without interruption. 'We have the behaviour management plan [posted
on the wall] and a new teacher looks at this and says "sit by yourself"
and doesn't give you a chance.'

What did it feel like?

Throughout the course of each day of the student panels, we began to
build up a picture of what school felt like for many of the young people.
The children typically saw themselves as being at the bottom of the heap,
labelled by teachers as 'thick', 'stupid', not wanted in the school. Table
4.2 illustrates some of the fears and anxieties, the day-to-day experiences
and the hopes and aspirations. These views were expressed in the
drawings, as well as through discussions.

For many of the young people we interviewed, school was a profoundly
sad and depressing experience. The images and depictions were powerful,
suggesting 'I am very sad', 'stressed out', 'lonely,' 'depressed', 'on my own'.
Many of the images are bleak, picturing isolated children and shouting
teachers. A recurring image is of school as a prison from which children
continually try to escape.

Table 4.2 School was a sad and lonely experience

The anxieties	Worried about examinations
	Not getting detention
	Concerned about the parents' evening
	Worried because I've done no homework
The day-to-day experience	Often bored
	Tired because of the noise
	The teachers are shouting all the time
	Learning nothing
The hopes and aspirations	Making friends
	Getting good marks
	Going to school more often
	Getting to know the teachers well
	Doing well
	Meeting the targets
	Hoping to make a fresh start

The physical conditions of the school played a prominent part in the images: smelly lavatories featured in many drawings. School was depicted as rubbish. The authority figures (the teachers) loomed large and seemed to have few connections with the young people on a personal level or through classroom interactions (see Fig. 4.2). The children themselves often appeared as lost, small voices crying for help, caught in a cycle of events and circumstances which they felt largely unable to influence. Once they had been labelled as difficult, once they were on the downward spiral of bad behaviour, conflict with teachers or truancy, it was difficult to escape. Their alienation was increased by a feeling that teachers and head-teachers wanted to 'get them out' of school.

Many pupils were deeply offended by the day-to-day physical environment which they encountered. 'The toilets are disgusting, they stink', 'there's no paper', 'it's horrible and unhygienic', were typical comments and occurred as images in their depictions of school life. Many described the dining area as being uncongenial and unwelcoming, 'It's really scruffy; the food is slopped on to a plate'. The poor physical school environment was interpreted as the school's lack of respect for pupils. 'They just don't care,' said one student.

Fig. 4.2 Watching the clock

What's school got to do with learning?

A common feeling expressed by many of the students we talked to was that 'learning' was boring. When probed about their definition of 'boring', a number of students defined that as 'doing the same thing over and over again', 'copying things off the board', 'not having any purpose', 'not being taught properly'. Almost uniformly, students found few connections between what they encountered in school and what they were experiencing, or were likely to experience, outside of it. 'Why do we need to learn this I want to know?' one student asked with some emotion and almost anger, 'No one can tell me except, "'cos you have to".'

In discussing the purpose of school, relatively few could see many positive benefits, although several suggested that if they were in the 'right' courses, then it might be worthwhile. Those pupils who valued education tended to value it functionally – you got examinations that helped you get a job. There was little sense of the intrinsic worth of education, or of any notions of enrichment or preparation for life in the broadest sense. Few associated school as a place for growing, learning new information or expanding their future options. One male student depicted himself in a drawing as a mushroom (Figure 4.3), explaining to us that he was someone who hid in the background and grew very little. The teachers had to look hard to find him.

Fig. 4.3 Hiding under the mushroom

Schooling was described as a grim and painstaking experience which had to be got through (see Fig. 4.4). Hanging out with your mates was one of the few saving graces. Students tended to place a higher value on the social network and interactions that took place in school with friends on a short-term day-to-day basis, than on any long-term benefits of lessons, classes and school.

School provided the opportunity to see friends and 'muck about with your mates'. The social network operated both inside and outside school. Students who did not attend school or lessons admitted to doing so with other friends, 'When you bunk off, you've got your mates with you'. Friends provided one of the few highlights in what for many was an otherwise hostile climate. School was also a place where pupils (particularly if they were 'different' or gay) could be bullied or ridiculed by their peers, ostracized – a process which could be deeply painful.

School was something that 'you had to do', but did not necessarily need to do in order to find work or earn an income. The world of work was an option that immediately followed school. As one female explained, 'If I don't do well in school, I'll just find a job or go on the dole'. 'I don't need school or qualifications', another male student stated. 'School should end earlier so I can just start working.' Suggestions for more practical or additional activities outside school were met with little enthusiasm. One pupil said, 'Six hours of getting hassles from teachers is enough. Why go to activities to get more?' Few students mentioned the prospects of further or higher education, attending college or university.

What would make a difference?

We asked pupils to draw up a wish list of what needed to change. A summary of that list is shown in Chapter 7, Table 7.2. Two examples of pupils' comments are shown in Figures 4.5 and 4.6.

In one panel, students discussed the list and voted on the top three changes. The overwhelming majority of pupils voted to be provided with more help and support with schoolwork. Pupils thought that schools and teachers could change and improve. However, there were also students – at least one or two in each of the five panels – who did not believe that any changes for the better were possible. However, when asked if there was anything they would change in themselves, many pupils stated that they would like to change their own behaviour, but they found this difficult because they had been labelled as 'the awkward squad'. One Year 10 boy concluded morosely, 'It's too late for me'. Other students said they

Fig 4.4 Stressed out

would like to try and deal with the problems with their teachers better. 'If I have a daughter', one girl said, 'I would tell her not to say anything to the teacher, but to tell me and I would talk to him or her.'

How others see it

One reference point for our pupil panels was a series of truancy panels which had been held in Lancashire in 1998.[2] The students who were persistent truants gave bleak accounts, not only of school life, but also of the boredom and frustrations of truanting. They described school lessons as 'boring' or 'dull', and spoke about being bullied and made to feel 'thick

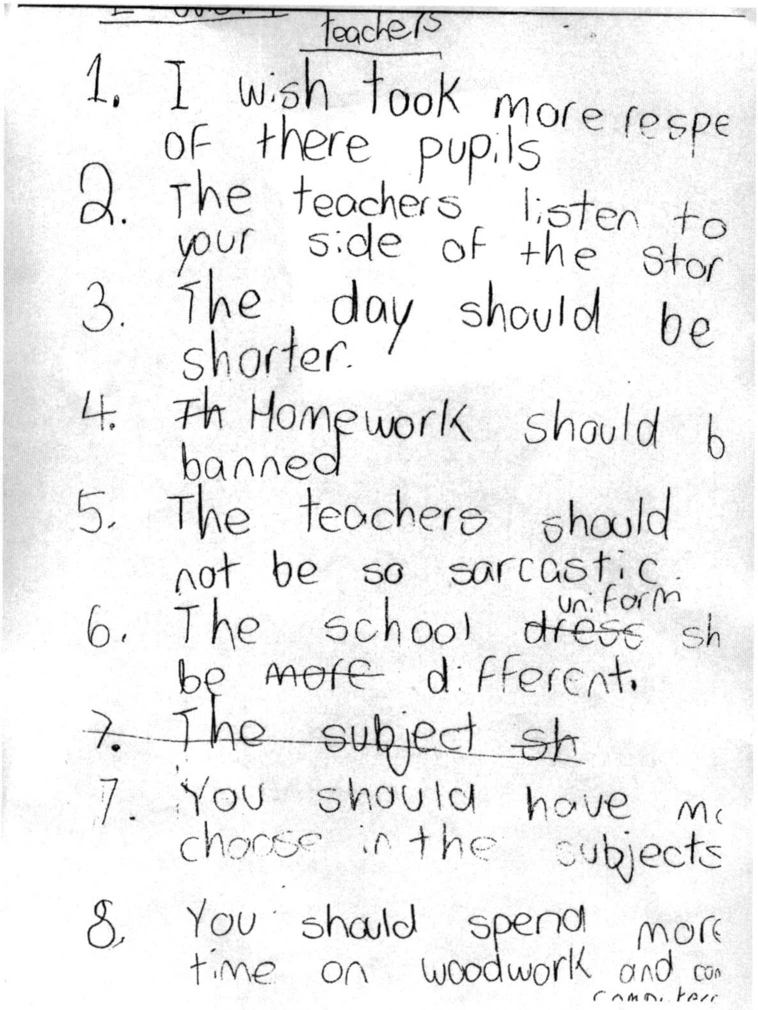

teachers

1. I wish took more respe of there pupils

2. The teachers listen to your side of the stor

3. The day should be shorter.

4. Th Homework should b banned

5. The teachers should not be so sarcastic.

6. The school dress uniform sh be more different.

7. The subject sh

7. You should have m chorse in the subjects

8. You should spend more time on woodwork and com comp. tecc

Fig. 4.5 I wish

or stupid' by other pupils as well as by some teachers. Most compelling were the personal accounts of their difficulties (perceived and experienced) in attempting to return to school (UNISON and the National Association of Social Workers in Education, 1998). On the basis of the evidence collected, panel members concluded that schools were simply not equipped to deal with the returning truant. Not only would effective monitoring systems be needed to track young people, but also more fun-

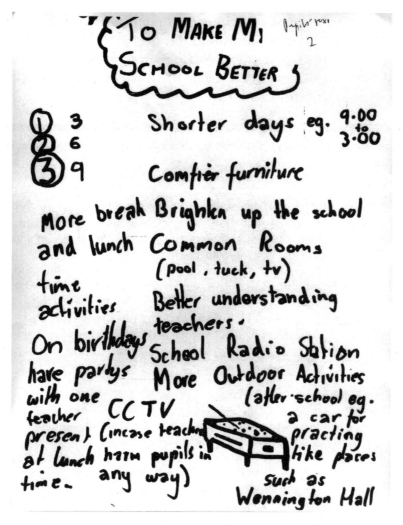

Fig. 4.6 To make my school better

damental changes would need to be made to many schools in order to reduce the incidence of truanting in the first place. Schools would need to become participative and child-friendly places that offered young people a lively and challenging curriculum.

Although our panels were somewhat broader and included a range of young people, not just truants, our findings were broadly similar. The findings from both sets of panels highlighted the day-to-day factors which blocked learning, including the impact of pupil–teacher interactions.[3] We asked our colleagues from Lancashire who worked with us on the student panels to write their perceptions of the three main issues which had emerged from the panels. We conclude this chapter with two examples of those accounts, shown in Box 4.1.

Box 4.1 The pupils' story: how some educational professionals saw it

Account 1: Female Education Welfare Officer (EWO)

- The main point that will stay with me is the fact that many of the young people recognize that their behaviour needs to change but cannot envisage the process of being able to change. Their behaviour is based on how staff expect them to behave.
- There is a major problem of communication between families and schools, but no one appears to recognize the problems, or be able to assist.
- The whole group had major communications problems with the teaching staff. They felt that teachers gave orders, did not treat them as individuals and did not give then any space to be able to discuss their problems.

Account 2 - Male Education Welfare Officer

- *Relationships.* Personal relationships between pupils and teachers are key. Time is needed to develop relationships and to build mutual respect. There is a recognition of the difficulties on both sides. Pupils might well understand the pressure teachers work under. We certainly saw evidence that pupils were aware of financial issues.
- *The importance of the physical environment.* There is a message about the low level of respect accorded to the pupils. They're not seeking luxury, just toilets and furniture that are clean, whole and appropriate. There is a strong awareness of the differences between schools, especially where they are close and are drawing from the same or similar communities.
- *Families.* There is a high percentage of parents who had truanted themselves and only mothers were seen as interested in, or responsible for, their children's education. Some young people expressed surprise that we asked about fathers. There is a recognition that parents have little power over them and that it is unfair for parents to be 'harassed' by the EWO and courts.

5

Parents' voices

'No Parents Beyond this Point' was a notice found in many schools in the mid-1960s, according to the Plowden Committee on primary education.[1] The committee concluded that the sign reflected an attitude of mind towards parents that needed to change. One goal of their final report was to encourage schools to see parents in a new light, and to involve them in their children's schooling.

Has anything changed in thinking about parents and schools over the intervening almost half a century? Certainly parents have been given more rights and responsibilities (Riley, 1998a). We know that parents play a key role in how their children experience or interpret school. We know, too, from research and practice that in 'good' schools, the home–school partnership works successfully (Riley, 2001). But how typical are such partnerships and what do they mean in practice?

Whilst a desire to involve parents in their child's education is common across many countries, there are marked differences in the ways in which that relationship is enshrined in legislation and interpreted in practice. English legislation emphasizes the *duty* of parents to educate their children. Danish legislation puts the child at the centre, depicting a partnership in which schools work 'in co-operation with parents, to offer possibilities for the children to acquire knowledge and skills, working methods and forms of expression which contribute to the all-round development of the individual child' (Foleskole Act of 1993, article 1.1; quoted in MacBeath et al., 1996, p. 226). Parents and schools are expected to work together to promote the child's growth and learning, and are seen as co-educators.

In the UK, current policies and practices in relation to parents vary between schools, and whilst there are many examples of good school–parent partnerships, the parent–school relationship is a fragile one. There are still many situations in which parents – particularly those of disaffected children – feel marginalized.[2] In this chapter, we look at the experiences of some of those parents.

We interviewed 18 parents in small groups, or through individual interviews. Twelve had children in two of the projects we had already reviewed in Lancashire, four were traveller parents, and all but one was female. We wanted to try and understand their beliefs and expectations about schools and education, their views about how the schools had responded to them as parents and their perceptions of their child's school experience.

We begin our discussion of the school–parent relationship by looking at it from the pupil perspective. Although we had not set out to probe this issue, it became a topic for heated debate and discussion. Their foremost concern was that of labelling. Some pupils thought that teachers viewed them negatively because of a parent's or a sibling's previous difficult history with the school. Others felt that their own attitude to school had been coloured by the negative experiences of their family members. One girl, for example, told us that her negative view of school was a direct reflection of the experiences of her mother, explaining, 'My mum didn't like school, and I am just like her'. Most pupils did not believe that their parents and family should be held responsible for their own behaviour and many expressed anger and frustration that parents should be held accountable for their attendance. A typical comment was, 'It is not right or fair to punish my mum for what I do … she has nothing to do with whether or not I come to school' (Year 11 pupil).

However, pupils still looked to their parent(s) or principal carer as the main source of support. Most pupils felt that they could openly discuss their difficulties and problems about school with their mothers who were their primary advocates. The ideal scenario for resolving the problems they experienced in the school was one in which their parents were directly involved in discussions with teachers or the headteacher. However, this ideal scenario was one which most pupils also thought of as 'hard' and 'stressful' for their parent(s) and unlikely to happen, as their parents often felt intimidated by the headteacher and 'put off' by the attitude of teachers – a perception shared by parents. Pupils' and parents' views about the parent–school relationships are shown in Table 5.1.[3]

Table 5.1 The parent–school relationship

How pupils saw it	*How parents saw it*
• Parents are negatively labelled by school	• Parents thought the problems could have been averted
• Parents can shape pupils' attitude towards school	• Parents saw themselves as beingin a 'no win situation'
• Parents should not be held accountable for their child's actions	• Parents thought that punitive policies were sometimes counter-productive
• Pupils want parents to be involved in their education	• Parents felt they were seen as part of the problem, not part of the answer
• Pupils felt that parents were intimidated by school and teachers	

The parents we interviewed were not always clear about what had caused disaffection with school but believed that, in almost all cases, positive intervention could have occurred at an earlier stage to prevent problems from escalating or to tackle learning difficulties. Parents attributed their children's problems to a range of reasons, but mainly viewed them as behaviour problems associated with frustrations about learning. According to the parents, teachers saw that a child was misbehaving but did not look sufficiently into the problems: what the child brought into the school; whether the child had learning difficulties; or whether s/he was being bullied. When their children were in difficulties, the parents we inter-viewed wanted to be supportive, but the pathways open to them to do this were often unclear. Parents told us that they:

• were intimidated by the process and environment of schools;
• were often unsure about whom to go to when they had a problem;
• communicated mainly with school management, rather than classroom teachers;
• were not sure what they could do when a problem erupted:
• wanted to help, but did not know how to help, or whom to go to.

Whilst parents realized the school's limitation in terms of resources and pressures, they also gave compelling accounts of the process of labelling (of them and their children) and of schools' apparent hostility towards pupils. The parents, as the pupils themselves, could identify particular events that had triggered further bad behaviour on the part of their children and contributed to the downward spiral. For example, at various stages in one panel discussion, one mother pieced together her painful story about her son which is described in Box 5.1. Her son, now in secondary school, was still struggling, unable to overcome the label of stupid and thick which had bedevilled his school career.

Box 5.1 'He never liked school from that point'

The teacher put a label on his back, 'Don't talk to this boy, he bites'. He was six at the time. He didn't want to go to school … She had a stack of notices and she kept them near her desk, but you couldn't see them when you went into the classroom … I spoke to the headteacher and he spoke to my lad in assembly. He made him stand up. He said, 'Your mum doesn't want you to have a label on, but it's up to you to behave!' … The problem was he couldn't read, but they made him feel stupid. When he was nine, they said he was dyslexic but he had no help for a long time … The teacher who did that to him finally went from the school, but it wasn't because of what she did to my lad.

The parents we interviewed were clear that schools needed to take appropriate sanctions, but felt that some schools had adopted punishment regimes that were unduly punitive and did not encourage children to take responsibility for their own behaviour. Whilst these policies might work in the short term, in the long term they did little to alleviate the deep-rooted problems and could exacerbate resentments. A particular example given was the 'isolation policy' that had been introduced by a number of schools. Pupils who misbehaved consistently were put in isolation (or 'ice' as many of the pupils referred to it in their interviews and in their drawings – Figure 5.1). Pupils in 'ice' were separated from other students throughout the school day. One mother's critical views of the isolation policy (or 'ice' policy as our pupil panellists described it) are shown in Box 5.2.

Fig. 5.1. The 'ice' policy

Box 5.2 The 'ice' policy: a parent's perspective

I went up to the school. He was in isolation in a tiny room on his own. I said to them, 'You can't put him in here, it is like a prison' … You have got to punish them, but not like that … Make them clear the rubbish from the playground or not play football if they act like that … The isolation policy doesn't help. When they miss lessons, they feel even more of a problem.

They never had anything good to say about him, no matter how small. Parent evenings were terrible. Them and us! I thought the days of boot camp had ended, but when I got to the school I saw the way they dealt with him in isolation – it was every bit as bad.

According to several mothers, the punitive and unhelpful approach adopted by the schools put them on the defensive and contributed to the history of poor relationships between schools and parents. As schools only saw the boys in a negative light, the mothers felt that they had to speak up for their sons:

> What they didn't understand is that when they knock him down and don't say anything good about him, all you can do is speak up for him ... They don't see that they have any responsibility for what has happened.

The parents, particularly those mothers who were single parents, felt that they were seen by the school as part of the problem which needed to be 'sorted'. In their view, the single-parent label was still a stigma and contributed to the negative views that the school had about them. Fathers were often seen as being peripheral to the problem and, according to the mothers we interviewed, in practice often were so.

Despite these problems, there were policies and practices which could make a difference for parents. These included specific facilities (such as parents' rooms), working arrangements (such as home visits by teachers), particular approaches (such as empathetic attitudes and non-judgemental views of teachers), and successful projects (such as Parents as Educators which brought parents into schools, developing their skills and providing them with important insights about schooling).

6

Teachers and headteachers in the firing line

In the closing days of the 1939–45 war, Arnold McNair was given the task by the Churchill government of looking at the supply, recruitment and training of teachers. The McNair Report concluded that the teaching profession would need to be made more attractive and its status enhanced as 'England, – we do not say England and Wales – has never attached enough importance to education and has therefore never given the teaching profession the esteem it deserves'. The report argued for a change of heart and emphasized the importance of teacher quality. If the country was to create a 'wise democracy' in the post-Hitler world, then it would need to recruit people of the highest calibre to teaching. The ban on married women teachers (which had been imposed by many local authorities) should be reversed, as it resulted in the loss of a highly qualified and dedicated group of teachers. Teaching required more than knowledge of subject matter. Teachers needed to be able to interpret the meaning of complex changes and enable young people to be able to discriminate and not be 'an easy prey to sensations and cheap appeals'. The report concluded that the teaching profession had a strong social purpose and needed to be at the heart of the post-war reconstruction of society (Riley, 1998a).

Over recent years we have witnessed growing demands and expectations of teachers and greater demands for accountability. Teachers often find themselves caught in the firing lines: managing competing and growing pressures. In carrying out our interviews with teachers and headteachers, we wanted to understand those pressures and what could be done to tackle them. Although we found many frustrations and problems, we also found a yearning to do things differently. Teachers wanted to be the teachers that they came into teaching to be, to rediscover old skills and to discover new ones. Headteachers wanted to think of themselves as lead educators, responsible for the intellectual as well as the daily welfare of the students, teachers and other paraprofessionals in their school.[1] We started our discussions by looking at the nature of the problem of student disaffection and asking the question – *Is it down to home or school?*

Home or school?

The causes of disaffection were seen as originating from, and being reinforced by, home and parental factors: a perception familiar in the research literature. Factors mentioned included poor parenting, disordered home life, family break-up and negative parental attitudes towards school and education that sometimes stemmed from parents' own unhappy experiences of school. A lack of support from parents was mentioned as a particular barrier to learning. Staff described the difficulties they experienced in trying to communicate with parents, and the variety of means used (including phone calls and home visits), but felt they could do little when a parent refused to co-operate. They saw themselves as being particularly powerless in the face of high levels of unemployment and community deprivation. (Headteachers' and teachers' views about these issues are shown in Table 6.1.)

Whilst headteachers recognized the crucial role of parents, they were concerned about the anti-education approach of some. 'A generation of parents coming through are anti-school', lamented one interviewee. 'They give no support to school and are prepared to challenge and always take the pupil's side – and the pupil knows this.' Such attitudes, coupled with the limited opportunities for employment facing many disaffected pupils, contributed to an anti-education culture and an inability to see any meaning in the future. Headteachers also felt that the parents of disaffected young people often had little understanding of their children and were frequently unable to support them emotionally.

Despite the problems that pupils experienced at home, headteachers and teachers thought that schools could make a difference. However, the introduction of competition and league tables, with all their additional pressures on teachers, had combined to create inappropriate demands on those pupils who had little interest in preparing for a world which did not interest them. Some headteachers argued for a move back to a 1980s vocational curriculum and suggested that there were far too many students in the lower ability range following courses which were unsuitable, irrelevant or inappropriate. Secondary headteachers emphasized the need to provide a curriculum which would meet the interests and needs of those pupils. Several reported success in winning back the interest and involvement of some students. 'Extended work experience is brilliant' was one comment, echoed by another headteacher, 'Yes I'd agree. That and GNVQ [General National Vocational Qualification] ... They have really helped to improved attendance, but they're not a panacea for everything.'

Table 6.1 Home or school?

How headteachers see it	How teachers see it
Is it the home?	*Is it the home?*
Schools can provide what many homes cannot – stability, security, consistency, a clear set of parameters. ... We can see children who behave in a thoroughly civilized way in school but act like thugs out on the street.	Often the parents will call *us* asking for help with their child. When we experience difficulty with pupils, it is almost always the case that the child's parent is having difficulty at home. Parents in schools like ours have little or no understanding of how complex children are.
For some (parents) education is not only not valued but seen as an encumbrance – it can prevent all sorts of useful things like shopping and staying in with parents, getting to work and bringing money into the family.	Any talk of education as preparation for life has no meaning [for the parents of disaffected children] and no meaning for their children.
Is it the school?	*Is it the school?*
There is much we can do in terms of offering an accessible curriculum, supportive teaching, and personal support. The GCSE curriculum and national targets are also a problem. There's a lot of labelling of pupils but it is subtle, and hard to confront when it is your colleague.	Sending a pupil out of the classroom can just reinforce their belief that they are thick and unwanted, but I feel that I have to do it because I have others to teach. There is one (disaffected teacher) in every school . . You know who they are, and you're not sure why they are teaching. I can think of one

teacher in our school, and she just doesn't like children. And I feel sorry for her students. ... I wouldn't want to be in her class.

What are the signs?
Some nursery staff and governors can predict problems ten years down the line. They can see [the problem] when the children come through the door.

The warning signs (of disaffection) are restlessness, a lack of interest in schoolwork, difficulty with homework and a lack of personal organization.

What are the signs?
By the time these kids get to us (in secondary school)... it is already too late ... These kids need a lot more support than we have time to give because we have to get on with the curriculum, and preparing the rest [of the pupils] for exams ... As a result, these youngsters slip through the cracks.

Expectations and attitudes were key and the connections between labelling and disaffection strong. However, labelling was difficult to detect and confront, and those headteachers who recognized that an inappropriate curriculum and poor pedagogy could aggravate disaffection also saw the impact of labelling on students, and their parents.

Most of the headteachers we interviewed said they tried hard to avoid negative labelling and encourage staff, pupils and parents to have high expectations of pupil achievement, but as one conceded, 'Changing expectations is hard when you've been seen as a low achieving school for so long'. Headteachers had to try and raise the expectations of their staff but this was sometimes difficult. One headteacher was concerned, for example, that staff thought her expectations were too high, 'I said no, they're not because if you look, we're compared with like schools and they're doing considerably better ... But it's very, very difficult to turn their perceptions round as they are feeling extremely overworked and I'm just adding more pressure.'

Problems and solutions

Identifying the problem is the easy part

In order to gain some understanding of the stages and phases of disaffection, we interviewed primary as well as secondary teachers. According to our primary interviewees many children, described by their teachers as being disaffected seemed able to cope in a primary school environment but then struggled in a secondary situation. Although disaffected behaviour was exhibited at the primary level, the problems become more acute and seemingly intractable in a secondary environment. A number of explanations were offered for this including:

- *school size* (secondary schools are usually larger than primary and the structure could be overwhelming, especially for the disaffected pupil who needed extra support);
- *number of teachers* (pupils encounter many different teachers during the course of their school day);
- *lack of personal attention* (because of the nature of the secondary school, less individual attention is typically paid to pupils' personal and emotional needs);
- *other children's attitude* (in the secondary environment peer group pressures are strong and pupils can become subject to bullying, especially from older pupils, and to a range of negative influences);
- *the contrast between primary and secondary school approaches to learning* (primary approaches are seen as focusing on a child's needs, whilst secondary school approaches are seen as being more subject orientated).

Primary teachers thought that they could tell 'right away' whether a child was at risk of disaffection. Children were often 'tired', 'confused', 'not happy'. However, once a problem had been identified, there were delays in receiving support in what was seen as an overly bureaucratic process. Teachers had to keep 'calling and calling' until someone finally responded, but by then it was often too late – the child had usually done something drastic or the situation had moved from prevention to crisis. Primary teachers also commented on the overwhelming amount of paperwork needed, once a child had been identified as struggling, and on the time pressures and further delays created by this. However, once help was received, this was appreciated and teachers were particularly warm in their comments about the Education Welfare Service, although they also saw it as being very overstretched and gave anecdotes about staff leaving and the problems of sick leave and lack of cover.

According to both to headteachers and teachers, disaffection manifested itself at different stages and in a number of ways. Many saw the most visible signs and symptoms as anti-social behaviour and aggressive anti-establishment attitudes which masked a deeper anxiety and uncertainty on the part of disengaged pupils. Disaffection was seen as starting in the primary school for many pupils but 'hardening up' on transfer to secondary. Low-ability pupils were thought to be particularly at risk and in need of additional help and support with a range of skills, including basic study skills, as well as support in reading and writing. Behaviour tended to be linked to non-involvement in school-based activities, both formal and informal. Typically, the disaffected 'give up even before trying', they 'start engaged and then become switched off'. Youngsters became non-attenders because they saw little point in being in school and found life more interesting in the wider world.

Although teachers and headteachers both from primary and secondary schools appeared to feel that schools could make an important difference in shaping the future prospects for disaffected young people, they saw the factors surrounding the problems of disaffection as being complex and multidimensional, and thus often beyond the school's influence, although the school had a role. As one headteacher put it, 'I think one of the frustrations we face is that some of the problems the children bring with them … are so great, and they trail so much baggage that there's only so much that we can do … and there's not a multi-agency approach to working with the youngster'.

Teachers and teaching

Uninspiring teaching and uncaring attitudes can lead to personality clashes and exacerbate the kinds of poor behaviour typical in disaffected pupils, which in its turn can lead to exclusion and truancy.

Teachers and teaching were seen as key factors that could make a critical difference for some disaffected youngsters. A wide range of imaginative teaching styles could help prevent disengagement from learning. Conversely, bad teaching could aggravate disaffection. According to one headteacher, teacher self-confidence was key and it was important that staff 'didn't take challenge and poor response personally'.

From a teacher's perspective, a range of issues (from negative attitudes, to limited teaching methods) aggravated the problems experienced by disaffected young people. One teacher observed that,

> Many schools have a number of disaffected staff – especially those ingrained in a style of delivery no longer relevant – they find it very difficult to cope with lack of respect and anti-establishment views.

Whilst primary school interviewees saw the problem of 'disaffected teachers' as largely being a secondary one, secondary teachers thought that teacher disaffection manifested itself differently in the two contexts. Both were united, however, in the view that disaffected teachers were a hard core who were 'difficult to move' and that it was 'hard to challenge their colleagues about how they chose to handle a disruptive student'.

According to our interviewees, the challenges at both secondary and primary level are great. Pupil behaviour is more testing than in the past and access to technology can change the balance of power between teacher and pupil. In response to these challenges, teachers needed to be innovative and willing to take risks. One headteacher opined:

> A willingness (for teachers) to take risks is important. Staff sometimes have to think of the most outlandish ways possible to teach their subject. But encouraging staff to develop a wide range of pedagogical skills is more difficult now – they are too exhausted to put their neck on the line.

We found a wide variance in how schools view and approach disaffection, and some schools are clearly more successful than others in tackling the issue. In general, there was a great desire amongst school practitioners to learn about and share elements of good practice with others, but schools found it difficult to balance the needs of disaffected pupils with those of other young people, particularly in an overly constrained work environment. All of the headteachers we interviewed were aware of the changes and improvements that could and must be made to win back disenfranchised pupils, such as earlier intervention and the development of strategies which could avoid precipitating confrontation. However, headteachers were also concerned about the needs of the majority of pupils whose learning could be disrupted by the challenging behaviour of their peers and sympathized with the concerns of many parents that 'problem children' should not be allowed to spoil life for the majority. In the final section of the chapter we look at the kinds of innovations, policies and practices teachers thought could make a difference.

What seems to be working?

Teachers and headteachers offered a number of strategies which they believed had been effective in helping to tackle disaffection. Some of these were internal to the school's organization, whilst others involved outside organizations and agencies. In general, schools appear to employ a range of strategies around the following areas:

- providing more individualized support to students;
- re-examining school structures, systems, and policies;
- improving the quality of teaching and learning;
- introducing counselling, mentoring and in-school support centres.

Schools that had developed a complex structure and network of layered support for teachers appear to have experienced the greatest success in addressing the needs of disaffected young people, and report more success in preventing exclusions. In addition, those who believe they need to adapt their practices to meet the needs of individual pupils are also the most optimistic about their ability to reduce disaffection.

Teachers particularly welcomed strategies which enabled them to spend more time with pupils. For primary teachers, the support provided by classroom assistants and by parents themselves was important. In primary classes of typically 30+ finding the time to focus on the individual pupil is an aspiration, although rarely a reality. The goal for the primary school teachers was to create a learning environment suited to every child's holistic needs. As one teacher said,

Every child, whether he or she is disaffected or not . . . needs to have an individualized learning plan, which includes the extra support that he or she needs, whether it is counselling or otherwise.

Curriculum and pedagogy

Several of the headteachers we interviewed spoke positively about the ways in which their schools had made changes to the curriculum and pedagogy to meet the needs of individual students whose experience of the school's standard offering had been one of failure and rejection. The introduction of national vocational qualifications with extended work experience had worked well in a number of schools. Some schools had taken further steps, including changes to the option system, extended links with tertiary colleges, expanded work experience and the introduction of flexible timetables for pupils. Curriculum was a key factor. Many teachers and headteachers thought that the academic curriculum and targets for national exams were inappropriate, and that the curriculum needed modification.

Counselling and support

A number of schools had developed counselling and mentoring opportunities for their pupils, using governors, members of the business community and peers (secondary school pupils linked to primary) as mentors. The success of counselling was confirmed by one headteacher who said, 'The most successful approach is individual counselling – via external counsellors – not part of the school but personal counselling'. Peer counselling was seen as a successful strategy, at primary as well as secondary level. Alongside these, external counsellors and mentors had made significant contributions. Headteachers spoke of the value of a home–school liaison officer: a 'neutral' person who could help build up a positive relationship with those parents who had an in-built resistance to dealing with school staff. One successful development was described as a pupil *support* centre, rather than a pupil *referral* unit. The intention was to remove the problem from the classroom and the ownership of the problem from the teacher. Another school had set up a learning support centre (funded from the Standards Fund) which catered mainly for students at risk of exclusion. Since its establishment, exclusion for Key Stage 3 (KS3) pupils had been reduced by two-thirds, although exclusions for KS4 pupils had remained static.

Several headteachers reported that the Single Regeneration Budget project, Raising Achievement, had been particularly valuable in working with 'targeted' pupils and establishing individual support programmes (see Chapter 8, Box 8.5). The involvement of other services, such as the Youth Service, had also produced positive results. However, headteachers were cautious about multi-agency projects, not because of the principle but because of the time commitments involved. In Chapter 8 we look further at the challenges presented by multi-agency working.

Rewards and punishment

Schools that reported success in addressing issues of disaffection appeared to have embraced whole-school change by re-examining behaviour policy, reconsidering how sanctions are used and making the pastoral system the core vehicle for support and communication.

Interviewees drew attention to the ways in which a school's behaviour policy can shape how disaffected pupils are treated and dealt with. Many teachers thought that assertive discipline policies were particularly effective in creating a positive approach to discipline. Rewards were seen by a majority of teachers as essential in helping improve the self-esteem of pupils and encourage positive change. Good pastoral support was cited as the most important area of support for disaffected pupils and seen as being 'absolutely critical' in helping staff to identify pupils' needs and communicate about their progress.

Common forms of punishments used in schools included lines, detention and removal from the classroom. However, many teachers indicated that such sanctions were not always effective in modifying the behaviour of disaffected pupils or helping them understand why they were being punished. For many teachers, the use of punishments appeared to be more about maintaining classroom control, and allowing teaching to continue, than about changing pupil attitudes or expectations – a view shared by parents. Teachers felt that, when using a punishment, it was critical to follow this up with the pupils quickly in order for them to understand their behaviour, but time constraints often made this difficult.

Training and professional development

For teachers, the call for inclusion meant that they needed to be better trained in using a wider range of teaching and learning strategies. Many thought that today's pupils had become more challenging and assertive, requiring from teachers a far more demanding set of skills than in the past. A range of teaching strategies were needed to meet the needs of pupils with challenging behaviour: a stand-and-deliver method of teaching was inappropriate.

Teachers, particularly the younger ones, felt that establishing trusting relationships between pupils and their teachers was critical, if disaffected pupils were to be re-engaged in learning. Mentoring was a key element of this strategy. For one teacher, the professional development which had been most successful in helping him improve his ability to teach disaffected pupils had focused on different styles of learning. Staff need 'high-quality training' one group of headteachers concurred. 'It is important for staff to talk to each other a great deal and think about their approaches', said one headteacher. 'It is inevitable that in schools like ours, staff are continually thinking about teaching strategies because if they didn't', another commented, 'the kids would be climbing out of the windows.'

Constraints and opportunities

The conflicting pressures generated by the twin agendas of league tables and inclusion were seen as constraining the development of a coherent policy towards pupils with challenging and disruptive behaviour. Both teachers and headteachers shared a concern that the pressure of government initiatives had left staff with little time to 'listen' to pupils and respond to their problems, or to share ideas about success with colleagues in their own or other schools.

The reduced role of the local education authority was also seen as a major cause for concern. Whilst headteachers welcomed many aspects of increased devolution of funds to schools, they were also concerned about their capacity to fill roles which had previously been met through local education authority services, particularly in relation to children on the margins. There was common agreement that the local education authority had a key role to play in tackling disaffection by:

- providing a lead in tackling disaffection through good information about current developments in this field;
- helping to encourage more networking and links between schools to enhance the exchange of good practice;
- helping to provide expertise and information on good practice available at a regional or national level.

Part IV
Policy and Practice in Social Inclusion

7

Different voices but similar tales

Listening to the different 'voices' in Lancashire has been a salutary and revealing experience. It has unearthed the frustration and mistrust between disaffected students and their teachers, and between teachers and the parents of those pupils. At the same time, it has also demonstrated a commonality of perceptions about what needs to be done – and how, and a commitment and enthusiasm on the part of many professionals to make those changes happen.

The parents of disengaged young people, and the pupils themselves in our study, had many common concerns and perceptions. Parents saw the punitive practices of schools, and the attitudes of teachers, as the biggest barriers and challenges to re-engaging their children in learning. What parents experienced as closed and unfriendly communications with schools contributed to a sense of lack of trust on both sides. Teachers had many similar concerns, recognizing that punishments were used to maintain classroom control rather than change pupils' attitudes or expectations.

Pupils were typically dissatisfied with the process and environment of their school (which they described in terms of the physical environment, as well as the teaching and learning which took place in classrooms). They demonstrated a lack of interest in, and disengagement with, the received curriculum. This disengagement was aggravated by a frustration with traditional styles and methods of teaching. Marginalized pupils typically experienced negative labelling and conflict-ridden interactions with specific teachers and saw little connection between the application of school-based knowledge and the 'outside' world.

The factors which shape the responses and expectations of their teachers and headteachers are complex. Teachers and headteachers today are under enormous pressure. Headteachers have to respond to a competing range of external and internal demands. Teachers have little time for reflection. The pressure to meet the requirements of national testing and evaluation sits uneasily with the wish to engage the hearts and minds of all young people, whether aspiring or disaffected. How to meet the needs of a young person who has returned to school after a period of truancy, or how to develop more challenging teaching methods which will engage young people more effectively in their own learning, are issues that many teachers would wish to tackle, but may not always be in a position to do.

Our interviews with teachers revealed a number of salient issues. Behaviour policies were often complex and difficult to explain. They varied between and across schools with both positive and negative consequences: *positively*, variance could mean that policies were flexible, and could be applied differently in different situations; *negatively*, such variation created inconsistency and mixed responses which pupils found difficult to cope with. According to teachers, some students sought punishment to gain attention – from the school, or from their own parents. We also found that teachers found it hard to bridge the gap between schools and parents, whilst acknowledging that schools could be unwelcoming places for parents.

The teachers we interviewed concluded that a rewards-based culture was a far more appealing and effective strategy than the use of sanctions and punishments. However, they also thought that some colleagues might find that hard to embrace, partly because of lack of time. There is also the pressing problem of *disaffected teachers* i.e. those who, according to their colleagues, do not always treat pupils with respect. What is clear to us is that the configuration of difficult, marginalized or vulnerable pupils with this small core of disaffected teachers is a sure recipe for disaster.

So far in this section of the chapter we have highlighted the points of conflict and tension, but through listening to the different voices we have also came to understand the points of agreement about what matters, and about the strategies and priorities for change. There was much accord between pupils and their teachers and headteachers. Table 7.1, for example, shows some common conceptions about the qualities which make a 'good' teacher.

Table 7.1 A good teacher is someone who ...

How disaffected pupils see it ...	*How teachers and headteachers see it ...*
• Takes the time to explain material in-depth • Is friendly and personable • Is understanding and knows their subject well • Uses a variety of teaching styles and innovative approaches • Is fair and has equal standards and expectations for pupils, regardless of their test scores • Is willing to reward pupils for progress	• Sees pupils as individuals • Has empathy with pupils and understands their needs • Is able to relax when appropriate • Has a sense of humour • Is a good planner, but is also flexible • Is willing to take risks • Has self-confidence and does not take challenge and poor response personally

There is much agreement, too, about the priorities for change (see Table 7.2). According to teachers, professional development opportunities and the time and space to work with individual pupils are key. However, as a result of the increase in administrative duties, and the pressure from the curriculum and testing, teachers feel that they have little time to reflect on their practices, and limited opportunities to discuss with other colleagues those strategies which appear to be working, as well as those that do not. Both teachers and pupils welcome opportunities, such as mentoring, which enable them to focus on small groups of pupils. Paying closer attention to what is happening to individual students is a mutually *enabling* process which has huge payoffs for both pupils and teachers. It *enables teachers* to recognize and understand differences in learning styles and to address and adapt curriculum according to pupils' individual needs. It *enables students* to benefit from individual care and attention and to feel wanted, rather than rejected by their school.

Pupils outlined a range of strategies and areas of intervention that they felt had been helpful in reintegrating them back into school and re-engaging them in learning. These strategies were very similar to those suggested by teachers and included:

- skilled and innovative teaching;
- mentoring and supportive relationships with adults;
- academic support (particularly when they were struggling);
- a school environment based on rewards, not punishments.

Table 7.2 offers a blueprint for change – what needs to be done to improve schools and transform them into places in which disaffected children have some hope of flourishing – from the perspective of the groups we talked to. We have grouped the comments under a number of headings: diagnosis and intervention; structural changes; teacher–pupil relationships and school ethos; relationships between home and school; learning and the curriculum; and buildings and premises.

The young people's comments are taken from an aggregated list of the 'top ten' changes they would wish to see. From the pupils' perspective schools could be different, if they offered more choices, and if relationships between teachers and pupils were more equitable. Respect was key. Mutual respect needed to be shown in the classroom, teacher for pupil, as well as pupil for teacher. The physical environment which many children encountered on a daily basis – squalid toilets, poor standards of decoration – was a strong indication for many of them that they were not respected. In their turn, they respected neither the teachers, nor the school overall. The parents we interviewed desperately wanted their children to succeed, where they believed they had 'failed'. The commonalities across the group include: strengthened teacher–pupil relationships; greater focus on flexible approaches to learning; and the introduction of effective peer support, counselling and mentoring. The importance of the support, counselling and mentoring initiatives indicates the need to have individuals who can find a language which enables them to speak across the divides.

There are a number of structural, pedagogical and organizational changes which could be made to create a different learning experience for the disaffected young people with whom we talked and to enable teachers to approach their work in the ways which most of them would wish to. These changes include:

- *A recognition that for many children, schooling is a fragmented and disconnected process*: schools will need to build-in structural supports and arrangements to reduce fragmented learning and to ensure that

Table 7.2 Blueprint for change

	Pupils	Parents	Teachers	Other professionals
Diagnosis and intervention		• Earlier identification of the causes of misbehaviour and earlier intervention	• More professional development opportunities to enable them to recognize and understand differences in learning styles, and address and adapt curriculum according to pupils' individual needs • Tackling the problems of disaffected teachers	• Greater support for multidisciplinary working
Structural changes	• Smaller classes • More say for students in how schools are run	• An intermediary between schools and parents/pupils who can speak up for the pupils	• Counselling, peer support, mentoring opportunities for pupils • Greater opportunities for sharing practice within schools and across schools	• Increase the level of support available *within* school to support pupils (e.g. through school-based counselling, peer support) • Change schools' and teachers' practices to provide teachers with more opportunities to collaborate with each other
Teacher–pupil relationships and school ethos	• Teachers who listen to pupils rather than talk at them • Teachers who are more aware of the problems students face outside school • Encouragement for teachers and pupils to respect each other	• A more positive approach from schools towards students	• A rewards-based culture • More time and opportunities to work with individual pupils	• Personal relationships between pupils and teachers are key
Relationships between home and school		• Greater co-operation between parents, teachers and pupils to resolve problems • More frequent and more positive communications between parents, teachers and pupils		• Greater recognition of the difficulties parents face in dealing with schools
Learning and the curriculum	• Help with school work provided to pupils who had missed school • More informal ways of learning offered both inside and outside school • More challenging lessons	• Recognition that behaviour problems are often linked to learning difficulties	• More time with individual pupils • More flexible approaches to learning and the curriculum	• Provide pupils with a more encouraging and realistic view of their future (for example, through work experience)
Buildings and premises	• Improved physical conditions			• Deal with the basics: toilets and furniture that are clean, whole and appropriate

children who return to school after a period of absence, for whatever reason, are welcomed and catered for.

- *Increased emphasis on students' sense of lifelong learning*: this raises important questions about whether nurturing the notion of lifelong learning might improve the motivation of young people to attend or stay in school, particularly for those students who see very few options for themselves. Solutions aimed at providing work-related experience are usually based on the assumption that such experiences provide students with incentives to attend school, but it appears that for some students, it is may be reinforcing the notion that school is actually a barrier to beginning work.

- *Addressing the demands on teachers and promoting skilled pedagogical practices*: teachers, pupils and parents recognize the growing demands and pressures on teachers. However, within this climate of mutual recognition, there are also frustrations. Pupils largely see themselves as passive agents in the learning process; parents feel that they are seen as part of the problem, rather than part of the solution; and teachers that they are caught out by conflicting pressures. Pupils recognized the many factors which could have an impact on their own approach to classroom learning. These included the ability of teachers to develop meaningful relationships with students, their pedagogical competence, their knowledge and enthusiasm for their subject, and the ways in which they interpreted the curriculum. In their view, teachers needed to be given more time to do the job better, and to have the opportunity to experience training opportunities geared at enabling them to develop their skills – a view supported by the teacher themselves.

- *Improving the communication between teachers, parents and other external and school-based professionals*: what has emerged strongly from all the panels is a need to improve communications between schools and parents. According to pupils and parents, many teachers are unaware of the social factors and home circumstances which can have such a profound impact on children's learning. According to teachers, much is being done to reach parents, but success is patchy. Our evidence also suggests that teachers may be unaware of the externally based initiatives which are aimed at tackling disaffection. This lack of connectivity between school-initiated and externally generated activities aimed at tackling disaffection reduces the opportunities for holistic and consistent practices to develop.

In the next chapter we look at the specific changes in policy and practice which are needed to create a different learning experience for disengaged students.

8

Policy into practice

Introduction

In this chapter we have made a number of proposals for both policy-makers and practitioners for changes which are likely to reduce pupil disaffection and disengagement. Our work in Lancashire has shown us that the genesis for reform and change in thinking and practice lies within schools and local agencies. The policy task is threefold:

- first, to tease out that thinking and practice;
- secondly, to refine approaches and test their wider applicability;
- finally, to work across the education system to support implementation.

In our view, a combined policy-maker/practitioner approach is far more effective than imposition from town hall, county hall or Whitehall.

Many of the suggestions we have put forward come from existing good practice, and from the creative thinking of those close to the issues.[1] To test their overall relevance and applicability, we put our proposals to a conference of some 80 secondary headteachers in Lancashire and we have included some of their feedback in this chapter.

We presented the broad outline of our findings from this study and asked them: was it a fair representation? Did they recognize the story as we told it? Were our proposals workable? The answer to all those questions was an enthusiastic yes, but that 'yes' was tinged with something else, a sense of frustration, a feeling that as headteachers – lead educators in their schools – they recognized the story, but felt hampered from taking some of the steps needed. The conference generated some interesting reflections on the part of several of the headteachers about their overall approach. One headteacher told us at the end of the day, 'I've got to call the Rottweilers off. I've really got to pull back and stop pushing my teachers just to achieve the targets. We've got to start talking about children and about learning.'

In putting forward these proposals we have not set out to define a rigid set of targets and steps that should be met, monitored and measured over a specified timeframe. Nor do we suggest a 'one-size-fits-all' approach. Instead, we have outlined priority actions and identified areas that individuals and groups, both in school and non-school setting, can look at from a range of roles and perspectives. Achieving inclusion will require shifting the attitudes not only of pupils and parents, but also of teachers and other professionals. Our starting point is to suggest that any local policy aimed at tackling disengagement needs to contain two overarching features:

- a recognition of the need to raise the levels of *awareness and understanding* about the diverse needs and experiences of disenfranchised young people (as individuals and as learners);
- a commitment towards improving the *practices of schools and agencies* in ways that will enable them to respond to the needs of disenfranchised young people, their parents and their communities.

Building flexible, local systems that encourage inclusion will be a long and hard process that needs to be undertaken in partnership. Partnership is key – within schools, school communities, across schools, and between schools and the range of organizations and agencies who can make a contribution.

Improving the awareness and understanding of schools, agencies, practitioners and professionals about students' experience of rejection and disengagement is a good starting point. It involves a system-wide and holistic approach which requires better training, increased professional development and ongoing forms of communication between all key stakeholders – parents, teachers, professionals working with schools, local policy-makers and pupils themselves. It also means that goals will need to be clarified and an ongoing process of monitoring and reflection introduced.

Networks between schools can help improve the dissemination of information and encourage the exchange of successful practices.

Proposals for action

We have made five sets of policy proposals and also suggested a number of priority actions that might be taken to support these proposals and the overarching policy goals.

1 Promote an inclusive teaching and learning culture – by examining pedagogy, adapting the curriculum, and building positive relationships between teachers and pupils.
2 Create structures for facilitating positive and open forms of communication between parents, schools, and local agencies.
3 Improve multi-agency collaboration between schools and local agencies.
4 Improve the quality and level of professional training and development.
5 Encourage all concerned to take responsibility.

Proposal 1: Promote an inclusive teaching and learning culture – by examining pedagogy, adapting the curriculum and building positive relationships between teachers and pupils.

Teacher-pupil relationships

One of the most powerful findings from our work is that teachers – through their style, methods, and personalities – can have a significant impact on young people's perceptions of learning, and their experiences in schools. This finding holds irrespective of student's age, gender and background. Young people's motivation for learning is enhanced by positive relationships with their teachers. The classes they are least likely to skip, and are most likely to enjoy, are those taught by teachers they like. Developing inclusive practices for disaffected children is not only about adapting the curriculum to respond to pupils' individual or special educational needs, but is also about building better teacher–pupil relationships. A major challenge for schools is how to help teachers to interact more positively with young people on a daily basis.

We are certainly not trying to suggest that if only teachers were friendlier with their pupils, all would be solved. A teacher's relationship and interaction with his or her pupils is a complex arena, dependent upon and shaped by a range of issues, including time, professional development, guidance and leadership from senior management, advice from other colleagues, as well as what the young people themselves bring to the situation. Although teachers must determine how to respond to and interact with pupils, a school's policies and ethos can exert a key influence on the nature of the pupil–teacher relationship.

A powerful vehicle for influencing the relationships between pupils and teachers lies in a school's policies toward behaviour, discipline and exclusion. As we have already suggested, practices and policies on these issues vary considerably between schools. Sanctions for disruptive behaviour and the use of rewards for good behaviour can range from severe forms of punishment (such as isolation in small room – see Chapter 5), to a more learner-centred model. Successful policies and approaches appear to be those which are clearly defined, and seen as fair. In Box 8.1 we provide an innovative approach to developing a school behaviour policy. In updating a behaviour policy that was over five years old, the staff in one school decided to rethink the school's approach to behaviour, including its behaviour policy. They began by developing a list of expectations for staff.

Box 8.1 Rewriting the school's behaviour policy[2]

Teachers should do all they can to:
Use humour.	It builds bridges.
Keep calm.	It reduces tension.
Listen.	It earns respect.

Teachers should do all they can to avoid:
Humiliating.	It breeds resentment.
Overreacting.	The problems will grow.
Blanket punishments.	The innocent will resent you.
Over-punishments.	Don't punish what can't be proved.
Sarcasm.	It damages your relationships.

Always apply school rules as positively as possible!

The key element in the approach outlined is mutual respect. The policy went on to define expectations about pupil behaviour. Many of the young people we worked with recognized that teachers 'deserve respect' but experienced school as being about following a set of rules which were skewed against them, in favour of teachers. In their view, rules were not only for pupils but also for teachers. The experience of our work suggests that inclusive schools have a set of goals, beliefs and values to which both staff and students can sign up.

Pedagogy and the curriculum

Pupils benefit and grow as learners – regardless of their ability and background – by being nurtured and supported by adults, and by being given access to a curriculum which is challenging and supportive of their needs. Achieving inclusion for disaffected young people depends as much on the content of what is taught and offered to them, as on the ways in which it is taught.

Examples of teaching enjoyed by disaffected young people, and perceived as effective by them, included those experiences where pupils were able to connect learning to their own lives and their expectations about their futures. Such positive experiences included informal discussions about 'real world' topics, school trips and project-oriented lessons. The teaching styles and methods that young people seemed to dislike most and which they described as 'boring' were those techniques and practices that were repetitive, rigid and did not cater for the diversity of learning styles which exist in any classroom. Completing worksheets and copying notes from the board were activities disliked the most. Although a number of young people recognized the need for a teacher to 'be in control', 'to stand up and tell us what to do' and 'to write on the board' – many also believed that teachers needed to be 'more human', 'less controlling' and to be willing to vary their methods 'to keep us interested'.

Inevitably, the National Curriculum has a major influence on teachers' methods and style. It influences expectations, structures and choices. We found that the problem of pupil disengagement with the curriculum surfaced particularly with the older pupils (Years 10 and 11), who described feelings of pressure, despair, hopelessness and intimidation which they attributed to their impending examinations. The fact that lessons become tightly focused around examination preparation and coursework in Years

10 and 11 has worrying implications for how to engage disaffected young people who see the curriculum as irrelevant to their lives. When young people see their own chances of success in the examinations hurdle race as minimal, and feel 'written off' by their teachers and their schools, there are few chances of moving forward (see Figure 10.1).

Issues relating to pedagogy and curriculum need to be viewed and addressed together. Both are linked to behaviour management, as an integral part of the student–teacher relationship. Evidence from the pupil panels suggests the current pace of the National Curriculum and the pressure for examination achievement pose a number of dilemmas for both teachers and students alike, particularly in relation to time. Pupils typically spoke about 'having to go too quickly', 'going too fast'. They complained about teachers who did 'not have time to explain things before moving on to the next thing'. In Table 8.1 we outline our teaching and learning proposals and headteachers' responses to them.

For learning to be meaningful and relevant – not just for young people at risk of exclusion but for all pupils – teachers and schools need to individualize learning. This is about creating a school environment which encourages teachers to use a range of teaching methods, and to adapt the curriculum to fit with the needs of all of their pupils. It is also about recognizing the specific areas in which pupils may be struggling and the need to build and foster an individualized teaching and learning relationship. Making learning accessible – so that pupils can grasp and understand concepts at their own individual level – cannot, however, simply be about finding alternatives to mainstream schooling.

Proposal 2: Create structures for facilitating positive and open forms of communication between parents, schools and local agencies

Parents and professionals (inside and outside of school) share a view that positive forms of communication are essential in tackling the problems associated with disaffection. However, our findings revealed that one of the biggest barriers to effective communication between parents and schools stems from deeply rooted views and assumptions about disenfranchised young people and their families. The young people and parents in our study experienced this as a process of negative stereotyping and

Table 8.1 Create an inclusive teaching and learning environment

Suggested priority actions include:	*What headteachers had to say*
√ *Develop in-school systems for providing pupils who are disruptive with help and support that is learning based.* Examples might include peer support, counselling, or homework clubs so that student do not become excluded from learning and can keep up with missed work.	• Strongly agree, but we need to change performance tables to reflect inclusion. • Entirely agree – but it has financial implications • You need to focus on peer support, counselling, teachers and learning methodologies, a rewards-based behaviour policy and celebrating a wide range of achievements. • We need to offer a flexible approach to pupils returning after long-term absence – gradual reintroduction with some support for catching up. This, of course, has resource implications.
√ *Adapt the curriculum. Make sure that it is accessible, appropriate, and relevant.* Provide multiple opportunities for pupils to enter and engage with the mainstream curriculum.	• For all this to happen the government needs to free up the National Curriculum, provide extra resources, and alter performance tables to widen our views about wider achievement. • You need an overt emphasis upon the wider/extra curriculum – which can provide significant elements of motivation and inclusion. It can also be part of a positive rewards culture.
√ *Encourage teachers to consider the role of pedagogy in managing behaviour,* and to use a range of teaching and learning strategies to respond to the diversity of pupils' abilities and needs.	• Essential for the success of any school is full agreement that pedagogy is the key – for all pupils, not just disenfranchised.
√ *Re-examine the school's behaviour policy,* ensure that it is not simply about sanctions, but offers rewards. Include expectations for *both* staff and pupils to improve and foster positive relationships.	• Including all members of the community is common sense in a good school. • Too often behaviour is controlled through assertive discipline which is totally negative and confrontational.
√ *Define achievement in its widest sense,* recognizing the diverse ways in which young people express learning and rewarding pupils for their progress, not just the 'standardized' measures.	• Many initiatives from government, such as OFSTED, militate against achieving this. • We aim to practise this widely and significantly – but unless, and until, government accepts this view through radically revised messages to parents (league tables), we have little chance of broadening local assessment. • It's not just about praise, but also about producing a culture of it's 'cool to work'. • All pupils have the right to a good education – up to the school to provide the environment for learning for each child.

labelling (which in its turn reinforced the communication gap between parents and schools). The parents of disaffected pupils felt that schools were unfriendly and unwelcoming places which always gave the bad news and never the good. Those teachers who tried to forge a different relationship with the parents of disaffected children found it difficult. Young people themselves often felt caught in the cross-fire of the conflicting perceptions which in its turn reinforced a negative perception of school and a defeatist attitude toward improvement. Nevertheless, we did find promising practices and examples from schools that had succeeded in developing positive forms of communication with parents. One example is shown in Box 8.2, 'Parents as Educators' – a Lancashire initiative.

Box 8.2 Encouraging parental involvement ('Parents as Educators')

'Parents as Educators' is an example of a successful LEA-based initiative that has helped break down the barriers between parents and schools. Through a course-based structure, parents are placed in the school and work closely with an assigned teacher. Parents develop a greater understanding of the demands of teaching and how the curriculum is structured. They become more knowledgeable about how schools work, and feel empowered to communicate with teachers and to become more directly involved in their own child's learning. At the end of the course, parents receive a qualification.

We also found that the headteachers of those schools which appeared to be most successful in reducing exclusion shared a common perception of parents – not just as interested individuals, but as 'equal partners' in their children's learning. Although such an approach was 'hard work' and required time and perseverance, headteachers and staff believed that it paid off and that a strong connection between the home and school lives of children could make a critical difference. An example of how one school took on those issues is shown in Box 8.3.

The suggestions we put forward to headteachers about improving communications were seen as practical and relevant to the challenges which

Box 8.3 Keeping exclusion low: the practices of one secondary school

Our work on exclusions in secondary schools in Lancashire found that in one low-excluding school, home visits were regularly conducted by teachers as a way of building trust and improving communications between parents and teachers. One newly qualified teacher at the school described her first visit to the home and community where one of her pupils lived as a 'professional turning point', one which had allowed her to understand the barriers faced by her pupils. 'Staff understanding and awareness of pupils' backgorund is not about socially labelling a pupil', she explained, 'but about being individually supportive and sensitive to pupils' needs.'

The school also used a team of school counsellors to provide pupils with additional emotional support. For one Year 10 male pupil, receiving counselling had prevented him from being excluded and helped him 'stay on track'. The young boy, whose parent had recently died, explained to us that through counselling, he had found someone to share his frustrations and this had helped him 'understand adults'. The school counsellors attributed the success of the programme to the style of the school's senior management as well as the commitment of teachers, with whom they communicated regularly. 'Counselling can't work by itself,' explained one counsellor, 'it needs to be accompanied by good teachers who are willing to understand pupils, too.'[3]

they and their staff schools faced. Other good practice examples were also offered by the headteachers, see Table 8.2.

Proposal 3: Improve multi-agency collaboration between schools and local agencies

Initiating system-wide change requires a shared and open commitment to partnership. However, a common problem faced by school (and non-school-based professionals) committed to multi-agency work is how to communicate information about students. The school staff we interviewed thought that professionals from other agencies were overburdened, and did not have the time for follow-up. Professionals from other services and agencies described similar problems in finding ways to communicate with teachers, and in monitoring a young person's progress in school.

Table 8.2 Create structures for positive and open communication

Suggested priority actions include:	What headteachers had to say
√ *Use varied approaches for communicating positively with parents.* This can include holding parents' evenings within the community and developing team-oriented ways of communicating with parents to lessen the burden on individual teachers.	• Crucial, we operate a pre-exclusion approach which includes a teacher mentor. • We try and do many of those things such as community meetings and regular newsletters, letters to parents on pupils' progress, i.e., targets met and not met. • 'Good News' postcards are effective. • You're right about developing positive communication with parents.
√ *Notifying parents when their child has made progress or shown improvement* has also been found to improve relations between parents and teachers. √ *Encourage parents to visit the school and to get actively involved.* Creating a parent or community room is a sign that parents are welcome in the schools and are seen as valued partners in their child's learning.	• (Other good practices include): link workers – not teachers – to work with parents and an open telephone line to headteachers – prior to 8.15 a.m. and after 5 p.m. • We run a crèche on parents' evenings so that parents can have very young children looked after while they see teachers. • Trying still to get more parents into school. • You need to build parents' confidence and self-esteem to encourage them to play a greater part in their child's education.
√ *Inviting parents to observe their own child in the school* is also a strategy that indicates to pupils that their behaviour and learning are being monitored and discussed by parents and teachers.	• There are practical realities involved in inviting parents into school to fit in with a particular timetable or lesson – either to share good work and progress. • Engaging and involving parents is an important recommendation – far more difficult to achieve in schools serving deprived areas. Still trying to! • Agree – however, we need more time – and strategies/funding to create better links with outside agencies. • Interesting and important recommendation but logistically difficult. • Teachers are also parents and have lives to live! Parents' evenings impose a heavy burden already.

• These are all important but there are many resources constraints.
• Funding is needed to share good practice, particularly with schools with similar contexts.

Our review of multi-agency initiatives (a part of this overall project) revealed that efforts to reduce disaffection were most successful where there was a system of sustained and regular contact between the school and the various agencies working with young people. A good example is described in Box 8.4, Group Intervention Panel (GRIP). For multi-agency responses to be effective, schools need to be open to change and willing to communicate with a range of professionals. Similarly, agencies and services can facilitate communication with schools by sharing information, expertise and providing structures and incentives for collaboration.

Box 8.4 Preventing youth offenders from re-offending: a multi-agency group intervention panel (GRIP)

One example of a successful multi-agency initiative that has been effective in reducing the number of repeating young offenders is GRIP (Group Intervention Panel). GRIP relies not simply on the notion of partnership, but on the information gained through the communication between agencies. GRIP is based on a multi-agency panel which consists of representatives from schools, education welfare, social services, and the police. The GRIP panel is informed whenever a young person receives a caution from the police. The panel then meets to discuss and review the young person's needs from a range of perspectives and to recommend a strategy for addressing the young person's academic, social and emotional needs. The progress of the young person is reviewed at each meeting of the panel.

However, what information is needed, by whom, and for what purposes can generate problems. Professionals working in both school and non-school contexts held differing views about what kinds of information would be useful to have about a pupil, and expressed concerns about confidentiality. Teachers described instances when a pupil had alerted them to a problem but as teachers, they did not have a clear vehicle or pathway for seeking help. Some teachers were unsure about whether information about pupil's family or personal problems would be helpful, especially if the matter was sensitive. However, the staff of one low-excluding school told us that knowing about a pupil's situation at home provided a context for understanding and interpreting the behaviour of a pupil and enabled them to be more responsive and sensitive. As one teacher commented,

'If I know that that child didn't spend the night at home, I am not going to get on his case for having a dirty uniform'.

As the social fabric of society becomes even more complex, the importance of effective interagency-working increases. For children on the margins, the issues are critical. Whilst the policy proposals in this area were welcomed by headteachers, they also generated some of the greatest concerns (see Table 8.3). Developing interagency working is one of the biggest local challenges.

Proposal 4: Improve the quality and level of professional training and development

Research studies conducted in the UK and internationally have long shown that teachers with higher levels of training and professional development are far more likely to use and develop practices that are responsive to individual pupils' needs than other teachers.[4] Yet a UK survey found that, nationally, little attention is given in teachers' initial training to critical areas such as home–school communication. 'Too often, it is assumed that the skills needed to manage the classroom and to support learning are the same as those needed for communicating with parents,' the report's authors concluded (ATL, 2000).

For any policy to be effective, those who are charged with implementing it must feel capable and equipped to achieve its goals. A critical step towards inclusion is recognizing the need to improve the skills and knowledge base of both school and non-school-based educators, and to give them greater awareness of the needs of disaffected young people – a critical issue for both initial and in-service professional development.

Our study found that teachers and other professionals want ongoing professional development which focuses on inclusive practices and strategies for teaching and learning. Improving training and professional development, however, is not about requiring all teachers and practitioners to take a one-step, one-stop course through which attitudes are hopefully transformed in the course of a week. High-quality professional development occurs when teachers are able to connect the attitudes and practices which prevent inclusion with their own practices, and when they feel able to incorporate new forms of knowledge into their school and classroom. Project involvement can be an excellent development oppor-

Table 8.3 Promote interagency working

Suggested priority actions include:	What headteachers had to say
√ *Encourage regional-based collaborations between agencies to improve awareness* of the wide range of health-, social- and school-related needs of young people who are at risk of exclusion, and who are already 'known in the system'.	• Support it in principle – but practical experience is that all agencies are so fully stretched that securing time for meaningful discussion is a major barrier. • Fine – but collaboration with agencies needs time commitments from schools that can impact negatively on the teaching and learning which is so crucial. • Multi-agency does not work. • Yes, but I already feel that the school is being left to 'prop up' the child in many cases. Multi-agency approach should not have to be initiated by the school. • Agree, but I suspect these are the most difficult set of recommendations to implement. It requires known links with the schools from all agencies – and much time! • Links with health authority (especially school nurse) are good. Contacts with Social Services are attempted, but are rarely productive. • This is the area which is usually most frail and breaks down most quickly. • I think we need to start talking about how these recommendations can be achieved. Too often solutions are driven by the agencies and schools do not have the time/resources to be fully involved. • Huge amounts of time wasted in trying to contact other agencies – other agencies lack accountability to schools and more importantly young people. • An emphasis upon agencies/specialist personnel to operate within the school environment whenever possible / appropriate – this would assist the spirit of inclusion. • It would be good to centralize professions in schools (e.g. EWOs, social workers, police workers).
√ *Facilitate focused sharing of information between agencies* to improve awareness and communication between professionals and schools.	• Other agencies are not really interested in schools – especially Social Services – they say we are a priority but there is little active involvement.

- Good recommendation, sadly this is a big area of weakness at present.
- This concerns me greatly.
- Regular meetings with EWO. We contact Social Services, but they never seem to contact us!
- Agree in principle – but the issues of accountability and responsibility need to be at the forefront of any such proposal.
- We are working to develop a 'one stop shop' weekly meeting between school staff – and external agencies in the area.

√ *Build ample resources for time and meetings into multi-agency projects.*

- Effective multi-agency working has massive implications for staff costs – time and personnel.
- Time and meetings – what a laugh! How will this be resourced?
- Time and resources are essential.
- Try to do this, but the scale and practicalities make this difficult – setting up multi-agency meetings can be very time-consuming.
- Are there additional steps that you think might help achieve this recommendation area?
- Specific funding to facilitate meetings could make a real practical difference.

√ *Help to streamline communications by encouraging schools and teachers to use email. Though face-to-face dialogue is productive, a number of teachers described feeling frustrated and needing quicker ways to pass on information.*

- Funding to develop ICT infrastructure within the school – to provide all teachers with email access.
- Email – not all teachers have access to a computer.
- Teachers recognize the possibilities of ICT but without the hardware / software to access this – to say nothing of training, things will not move forward.

---

tunity for teachers. One example of a successful national initiative implemented locally in secondary schools throughout Lancashire was the SRB – Raising Achievement – Enhancing Employability project, aspects of which are shown in Box 8.5.

Once again, as is shown in Table 8.4, headteachers strongly endorsed our proposals. The problems of implementation included how to enthuse older staff.

Box 8.5 The SRB Teacher Impact Group

As part of the evaluation strategy, an impact group was set up and facilitated by the programme's co-ordinator who, in partnership with a local university, encouraged the practitioners and professionals involved in the SRB schemes to share experiences and examine the benefits not only for students, but also for themselves. What was particularly rewarding for the practitioners directly involved in the project was that they were encouraged to develop flexible and multi-agency ways of working with underachieving pupils and also assess the impact of the various projects in their schools. At the end of two years, the Impact Group (which consisted of teachers, youth and community workers, careers officers and other representatives from local agencies and services) concluded together that changes made within the school appeared to have the most lasting benefits to pupils. Examples of practices seen as being particularly effective for promoting inclusion included teacher mentoring, peer counselling and student-led conferences and workshops.

Table 8.4 Improve training and development

Suggested priority actions include:	What headteachers had to say
√ Provide newly qualified teachers with in-school training for teaching pupils from a wide range of skills and backgrounds (e.g. with emotional and behaviour difficulties). To support this process, capacity building for teachers needs to be linked with initial training, the development of newly qualified teachers, as well as professional development opportunities. Changes need to take place in initial training, as well as professional development.	• Yes, but we also need high calibre trainers. • Where is the high-quality training? Where are the skilled practitioners and successful examples? We would gladly tap into these but have searched long and hard to find these for our staff. • Fully supported – provided this does not have an undue impact on removing teachers from timetabled classes. • An important recommendation that is supported by the whole school culture and ethos. • Absolutely vital. • Good induction programme for NQTs. Trying to find time to allow teachers to discuss pupils – rather than discussing administrative matters.

√ *Provide experienced teachers with continuous, high-quality professional development.* Our findings showed that the most effective forms of professional development are not always outside of school, but can occur through providing teachers with the time, resources, and opportunity within their own school to develop ways of monitoring the effects of changes on specific pupils, and to share experiences with colleagues and other professionals. Teachers in the SRB's Impact Group, for example, acknowledged that greater awareness of pupils' needs resulted from sharing information and progress with other colleagues (Box 8.5).

- Essential.
- Total support.
- Changing attitudes and perceptions of longest serving teachers is a difficult task.
- Opportunities to share knowledge are critical – both formal and informal.
- Ensure pedagogy is a target.
- Need to monitor progress using OFSTED Inclusion Inspection methods in a positive way.
- Involvement of learning support assistants in training and professional development – have begun this.

√ *Give teachers regular opportunities to follow up and share their knowledge with colleagues and to reflect on and discuss implications for the school.* In order for intensive training outside of school to be disseminated effectively, teachers must have the chance to consider the implications for their school together, with their colleagues. All this requires the provision of time and structured opportunities for discussion between teachers and other professionals and support staff.

- NQTs and 'newish' teachers are excellent – problems with 40s staff going nowhere.
- Need to use time wisely for colleagues to see how other staff deal with similar pupils and how pupils are motivated.
- Teachers visiting or even working in other schools to broaden experience – a trench mentality can develop.
- Share good practice by looking at the systems/good practices in other schools.
- Give schools a resident supply teacher/s who can release staff to do the 'quality' work – already have the good practice within our schools.
- Do not spend enough time celebrating good work/ideas.
- Programme of classroom observation – sharing good practice.
- Career breaks for experienced teachers?
- Possibility of working/shadowing in like and contrasting institutions.

- All of them are important – but finding it difficult due to lack of time, increasing bureaucracy and the speed of current changes.
- All of them, but not in enough depth/frequency as yet.

Table 8.5 Encourage all to take responsibility

Suggested priority actions include:	What headteachers had to say
√ *Develop a local-authority-wide charter that outlines the principles of the local commitment to inclusion, and encourage schools to take this on board. The development of this charter might include the views of parents, pupils, and teachers who might share practices and experiences, which have been effective in promoting inclusion and reducing disaffection.*	• Teachers, pupils and parents have to work together to create ownership. • Useful, we have home /school agreements – the charter would help – but would need funding to implement. • Important if there is to be consistency of practice – but a charter does not guarantee that. • Recommendation is fine – but it is the changing of attitudes that's difficult and yet so important.
√ *Form a local-authority-wide panel of parents, pupils, and teachers to review and assess in one, three and five years' time how much progress has been made. A review of progress by those voices who have a stake in the outcomes could help promote ownership and accountability for inclusion.*	• Needs to be a well thought out charter. • A worthwhile aim. • What impact will it have on schools, parents, pupils? • Danger that it could be big on words but short on action. • I endorse it. • Yes, let us all sing from the same hymn sheets, but support schools to develop their own relevant programmes appropriate to their circumstances. • Yes, but not a one size fits all model. • Keep it very brief as pages of writing will help no one – more paper, less effect.

Proposal 5: Encourage all concerned to take responsibility

The responsibility for inclusion does not rest on a single organization, institution or group of individuals. Bringing disenfranchised young people back into the frame is a shared responsibility, requiring combined action on the part of many – parents and young people, teachers and other professionals. Parents need to be encouraged to become involved in their child's schooling; young people to take charge of their own learning; and teachers to understand the experiences and expectations of disaffected children. All of this takes time, as does developing good working relationships with individuals, organizations and agencies, and creating a common belief in a local community about future possibilities. Much depends on trust – as well as time. Time is what policy-makers tend not to have.

Headteachers welcomed the proposals for encouraging shared responsibility and were particularly interested in the notion of a local-authority-wide charter (with agreed goals and ways of working) which schools would sign up to. The idea of a panel which included parents, pupils and teachers was also welcomed, but headteachers could see many potential problems. (see Table 8.5).

Despite the overwhelming support for the broad thrust of our proposals, headteachers felt a sense of frustration, summed up in the comments of one headteacher:

> Many of these recommendations we have tried to address in my current and previous schools – nothing suggested here is a surprise – we have recognised the importance of these intervention strategies for years, but where are the practicalities? Where are the good inclusive schools to give practical advice? Where will the funding come from? What will schools stop doing to enable us to embrace some of these? Why should we reinvent the wheel?

Policy-makers will need to be able to provide some practical answers to those questions.

9

Making changes happen

In this chapter we focus on what it means to create the policy foundation for social inclusion and the *how* of policy change: *how* do you go about making some of the changes needed at national, state, local system or school levels? We look at the kinds of activities, attitudes and approaches which are the most conducive to change. We have focused a whole chapter on these issues because of the implementation gap – between people's understanding of what needs to be done, and doing it. Creating the policy foundation for social inclusion (i.e. developing a policy framework which will 're-enfranchise' disaffected children and young people) means creating a framework through which the goals and meaning of inclusive practice can be understood by both policy-makers and practitioners.

The framework for such a policy does not comprise a set of nationally defined objectives and targets that schools, services, and agencies should strive to achieve. It needs to reflect localized goals and aspirations that are meaningful to parents, young people, schools, teachers and other professionals who work with young people and that reflect their differing needs. The proposals outlined in the previous chapter will not be achieved through the imposition of rigid quantifiable targets (although some of these are clearly important), but through changes in practices, beliefs and attitudes.

Creating the foundation for achieving this policy shift involves confronting the real experiences and day-to-day concerns of the voices that matter – those of young people, parents, teachers and practitioners. It also means breaking down the visible and invisible barriers that have combined to reinforce the exclusion of young people from learning, and from experiencing success.

As we have already suggested, it is far easier to identify the barriers to learning than break them down. Barriers are not only socially constructed, but are rooted deeply in individual perceptions and attitudes, as well as in social and organizational practices. There is a tendency to associate disenfranchised young people with a set of psychologically based, negative traits and characteristics, or to typecast a pupil who is disaffected from learning as deviant, damaged and uninterested in learning. Even today, the view persists that a pupil's social background is the primary cause of his or her problems in school and society. The reality of course, is far more complex and far-reaching.[1]

The tendency to blame the young person's social 'deficits' and to seek 'quick-fix' solutions often appears as the sub-text of many proposed solutions. 'Blaming' the parent or child, rather than trying to rethink the ways in which schools and other institutions respond and define the problem, is often the easiest solution. We recognize, only too well, that the problems facing young people who are disenfranchised might stem from, or be aggravated by, factors outside of school. There are many issues to do with poverty, health and employment, as well as family circumstances, which lie beyond the efforts of schools. However, the practices and perceptions of schools, agencies and organizations can make a crucial difference. The key challenges are:

- What changes can be made within school?
- What can practitioners do to help young people succeed against the odds?

As we have already argued in this book, there are many policies which can be reviewed – in relation to the curriculum, approaches to teaching and learning, and behaviour management. However, changes in practices also require changes in perceptions and behaviour: teachers about their disaffected pupils; pupils about their overworked teachers, and marginalized parents and harassed teachers about each other.

At the local level, policy goals for supporting inclusion need to focus on creating, developing and supporting flexible systems that will enable and encourage local practitioners and agencies to meet the educational needs of all children and young people, across all types of social and educational settings. The focus needs to be on building the local capacity for change and improvement: what can be done to give local educators insights which will enable them to reflect on their practices, to learn from each other and – where needed – to change. In this chapter we highlight the process of change and improvement, raising issues that are relevant to schools, as well as local and national education systems. We focus on four elements:

- clarifying our notions about change and improvement
- defining a clear vision and strategy
- identifying and evaluating what counts as success
- disseminating knowledge and building capacity.

Change and improvement

The successful management of change is a central element of any successful policy that seeks to make a lasting impact.[2] In the context of a successful policy on social inclusion, good relationships, partnerships and networks are key. Effective networking is characterized by positive relationships based on trust, co-operation and mutually shared benefits (Riley, 2000). Successful partnerships can lead to better integrated services, wider consultation and greater clarity over policy goals. Multi-agency approaches are a key element of this partnership and can provide an effective way of tackling disaffection by drawing on shared expertise and knowledge. However, as we discussed in Chapter 8, issues about time and resources currently make such an approach difficult to achieve, as does the overreliance on the commitment of specific individuals, rather than on system-wide changes in institutional practices.

We found during the course of our work that strategies aimed at tackling student disaffection tended to contain implicit notions about 'change', 'improvement' and 'success'. Those practices which appeared to be *least* effective were based on deficit models which assume that the causes and dynamics of disaffection lie solely within the child and his/her family. Such approaches rely on 'improving and fixing' the perceived deficits of pupils, mainly by providing them with 'rewards and incentives' to change their behaviour.

In the short term, rewards and incentives are likely to have a place in any change programme, and can help to reduce incidence of disaffection and disruptive behaviour, but on their own they are an incomplete tool. The potential for sustaining long-term improvement is limited where programmes rely solely on pupils' ability to change, and fail to recognize that agencies and professionals may also need to change.

In terms of long-term sustainability, the evidence from our work suggests that approaches aimed at changing the attitudes and practices of those individuals working with disaffected young people are far more likely to have a sustained impact than those which provide pupils with short-term support which disappears when funding runs out. Greater consideration also needs to be given to issues of institutional implementation (and to the management of change), and to the development of 'Exit' strategies aimed at ensuring that projects have a maximum impact on mainstream thinking and practice.

Many of the approaches to tackling pupil disengagement which we examined focused on pupil self-esteem. Whilst self-esteem is undoubtedly an issue – as is clearly evident in the negative images which many pupils have about themselves – the assumption that rewards and incentives will improve pupil self-esteem reflects a limited understanding of the conditions that facilitate improvement and success. The system indicators used to define success are typically those of reducing disruptive behaviour and improving attendance and examination scores. Whilst these issues are important, the indicators do not necessarily reveal improvements in practices, attitudes, beliefs and conditions towards learning which are more reliable indicators of long-term change. Practices that appear to be working most effectively assume a different view of change, improvement and success. They assume that:

- change is necessary and possible at all levels, and that activities need to focus on improving school-based practices, and creating more vehicles for communication and greater awareness amongst professionals about what can be achieved and how;
- change and improvement require a holistic view of pupils' needs, and the development of flexible learning arrangements;
- success should be broadly defined to include not only improvements in examination scores but also a recognition of pupils' other strengths and weaknesses;

- improvements in pupils' performance overall arise from improved conditions for teaching and learning. Thus the evidence of success needs to take into account institutional changes in professionals' practices, attitudes and beliefs.

This view about change and improvement has been reinforced for us by the findings from the pupil, parent and teacher panels described in earlier chapters.

In terms of thinking about the nature of the task, we also found that the development of a few, but simple and clear goals, linked to strategic objectives, work far better than overwhelming schools and teachers with a barrage of goals and targets. All too often, 'do it all' approaches are attempted. Achieving inclusion will not happen overnight. It is a step-by-step process through which practices can be improved upon, lessons learnt and success built over time.

Vision and strategy

The success of any social inclusion policy will depend, ultimately, on the will and capacity of schools and institutions to effect change. As we have already suggested, the development of a clear vision and strategy for achieving inclusion will depend not on the imposition of a uniform set of practices but on the development of a common philosophy about the meaning and impact of social inclusion. This is far from easy. There are competing assumptions: about how to motivate young people; about whether the most effective solutions for re-engaging young people disaffected from learning occur within schools or outside schools; and about whether students should be offered alternative curriculum, or vocational skills in non-school settings. The general debate tends to see low achievement as a consequence of a lack of self-discipline, self-motivation, self-esteem and self-confidence, but often fails to connect these issues to any school-related factors, or to the general context for learning.

Given the complexities, the local debate is critical if schools and agencies are to develop and embrace a shared set of values, as well as agreed changes in practice that can be sustained over time. However defined, policy goals will need to build on the experience and perceptions of all concerned, particularly those of young people themselves. These goals will need to promote and be based upon a partnership between schools, parents and communities, and linked to the policy goals of other agencies and services (e.g. social services, health, police), as well as the specific initiatives undertaken by those agencies.

Specific steps and activities that can contribute to the achievement of these long-term goals include:

- *Clarifying roles and expectations and discussing practices and approaches:* encouraging schools and agencies to 'sign up' to common goals and specific policy objectives, perhaps through the charter-mark type arrangement described in Chapter 8, might be one way forward. It could provide a unifying focus, as well as a common language to talk about the issues of social inclusion.
- *Balancing strategic direction with local responsiveness:* the corporate strategy in any local authority has a part to play in clarifying a vision and strategy for social inclusion; making connections between various initiatives, and providing opportunities for local solutions. A good and effective policy would identify what strategic objectives need to be set out at local level; what structural changes need to be made; and what local arrangements are best suited to co-ordinate local activities and share good practice.
- *Responding to national concerns and local agency priorities:* this is a difficult task, requiring flexibility, dynamism and creativity. Effective policies are organic (recognizing that both the local and national agendas are constantly shifting and changing). They also offer diverse incentives for changing practice which take into account the different ways in which professionals define success.
- *Monitoring the role of quality and access in achieving inclusion:* the challenge is to distinguish between access to schooling, and the quality of that experience (i.e. the ways in which teaching and learning can serve to include or exclude). An overall policy framework will need to draw on the characteristics of effective programmes and what is known about good practice. However, enthusiastic and hard-working practitioners, caught up in new policy ventures, often find it difficult to compare what is happening within their projects, with comparable developments elsewhere, or to answer the question: *how do you know what works?*

Identifying and evaluating what counts as success

It is hard to pinpoint and define clearly what counts as success in tackling student disaffection. Schools and other agencies are often overwhelmed by the number of projects in which they are involved and find it difficult to make comparisons with other institutions about ongoing work, or to evaluate the outcomes of particular projects or approaches. Project evaluation is often an 'add on' – something hard-pressed co-ordinators do to justify funding, or to measure some outcomes at the end of a project. Information from evaluations is rarely used to help change current practice, or to shape new policies or practices. Anxiety about evaluation, and pressure to produce 'results', create a tendency to collect readily identified, quantifiable indicators which may not necessarily indicate whether there have been significant changes in attitudes, expectations or aspirations.

Evaluation is a critical method for identifying the characteristics of effective programmes, but in general terms, it is an undeveloped area. Project evaluations tend to focus more on implementation than on assessing the achievement of goals and rely for evidence of impact on pro-fessional, rather than user, views. A focus on the user is likely to reveal, for example, that for many pupils, the most significant indicator of success is the development of close and trusting relationships with adults.

Evaluation is complex. Projects have a habit of changing and evolving over time for a range of reasons: the young people involved bring their own perceptions and experiences; new personnel become involved; new funding streams emerge; the project moves its location. The evolutionary nature of projects means that it is all too easy to lose sight of what the project first set out to achieve, and how, and the difficult-to-make decisions about replicability. Determining whether a project is working as intended requires a careful examination of issues of relapse and failure. The short-term relapse of an effort undertaken by teachers, for example, may not necessarily mean that the project or intervention is not working, but could be about constraints of time or resources.

There are a number of key ingredients for defining success and building future capacity. These include maximizing the long-term impact of evaluation and disseminating shared knowledge and practice. Long-term evaluations will need to ask such questions as:

- *Implementation*: was the innovation ever really implemented?
- *Fidelity*: once implemented, did the innovation maintain its original purpose? If not why not?
- *Impact*: have students been positively and significantly affected?
- *Institutionalisation*: did the innovation become integrated into the mission and organization?
- *Maintenance*: do successful programmes continue to exist?
- *Replication*: is it possible to transfer the innovation from one context to another? (Riley and Louis, 2000)

Disseminating knowledge and building capacity

To avoid the problem of reinventing the 'evaluation wheel', guidelines for good practice – both in terms of how internal evaluations might be carried out and how external evaluations might be commissioned – could serve to provide benchmarks for measuring success. As part of a strategy for disseminating project findings, an archive of completed evaluations would also make a significant contribution to the sharing of knowledge and understanding, including how to use evaluative tools.

To a large degree, disseminating knowledge about good practice will depend on whether schools and professionals are encouraged to share understandings about the practice of inclusion. A well thought-out dissemination policy can help develop capacity by increasing access to knowledge and information, not only for education professionals, but also for parents and students. If dissemination strategies are designed to ensure that information reaches schools and classrooms, then projects and initiatives will help to transform and change practice.

Dissemination is an integral part of capacity building and can take place through initial and ongoing professional development, as well as through involvement in new practice initiatives. As we have found from our work elsewhere, successful schools are those which make dissemination – from successful teaching and learning strategies, from projects, as well as from research – part of their daily practices (Riley et al., 2001). A 'good practice' chain which connects theory and practice and which includes incentives to share information and create workable and sustainable solutions is critical. Information technology can play an important part in this good practice chain. However, pressures to take on new initiatives, and the competitive climate, create obstacles to the sharing and dissemination of good practice.

We conclude this chapter by providing a template that can be adapted by practitioners and policy-makers to analyse and compare information about projects designed to tackle pupil disengagement (see Table 9.1). We have used this framework to help carry out audits of what is being done in a locality, as well as to help people think about evaluation.

Table 9.1 A framework for analysing approaches to tackling disaffection

Features	Key questions
1. Impetus	• Why was the project developed? • Is it a locally initiated response, a pilot project, a school-based approach or a national initiative?
2. Agency involvement	• Is it a single- or multi-agency effort? • Which agencies are involved?
3. Target population	• Which groups of young people does the project focus on? • How are participants identified, and by whom? • What information do they receive?
4. Project goals and scope	• What are the project goals? • How widespread is the scope of the project? • What activities and approaches are being used to achieve the project's goals? • What appear to be the assumptions (about reducing disaffection) which are behind the strategies being used?
5. Project support and training	• What kinds of support are being provided, and by whom? • What provision for training and development is offered to the practitioners and professional involved?
6. Project outcomes. Evaluation dissemination	• Is the project being evaluated, and if and so how? (self-evaluation/external evaluation)

- Does the project appear to be working?
- If so, what is the evidence for this?
- Does the project appear to be having an impact on participants and others?
- How is 'success' being defined in the project?
- Is information about the project being shared and disseminated? If so, how?

10

No more villains

Schooldays are unlikely to be the 'best days of your life' for all children, in all circumstances. However, there is compelling evidence to suggest that much more can be done to break the cycle of disaffection which creates barriers to learning for young people, not only in their schooldays, but beyond. There are lessons from our work on student disaffection for practice and for policy, and for the ways in which policies are developed and implemented.

American writer Seymour Sarason has argued that educational reforms tend to fail because they focus on the supposed villains of the piece, 'inadequate teachers, irresponsible parents, irrelevant or inadequate curricula, unmotivated students ... an improvement-defeating bureaucracy' (Sarason, 1990, p. 13), rather than on the educational system itself. Educational change, he argues, is unlikely to take place unless there is a fundamental alteration of power relations in the education system and in the classroom: a shift, which he describes as a necessary, although not sufficient, condition for improvement.

We agree with this analysis. A 'saints and sinners' approach to educational reform is a dead-end route. Children may be denied learning opportunities because of their own intransigence, or that of their parents. They may be 'turned off' schooling by disaffected teachers. We do not need to apportion blame, but to understand some of the causes of the problems and develop appropriate strategies. The sad and bitter experience of many of the young people we interviewed is apparent in what they said and drew, as for example in the vivid and disturbing picture drawn by a young woman which shows the sad crying eyes of a pupil and an escape ladder, out of reach in a chaotic and frightening world (see Fig. 10.1). What

matters is what can be done to ensure that young people are not disenfranchised and marginalized in an increasingly complex society: this is as

Fig. 10.1 No escape

important for society as a whole, as for the young people themselves.

Our findings suggest that for many children on the margins, schooling
is a deeply boring experience which can also be hazardous and demeaning.
By and large, this is not because teachers are uncommitted to the needs
of disaffected children, but because both teachers and pupils are locked
into an education system which gives them little room for manoeuvre.
The over-busy national policy agenda, characterized by repeated policy
waves, appears slow to learn the lessons from previous reforms and has a
tendency to mistake change for progress. Teachers have little influence on
the policy framework which shapes their lives. Some have greater opportunity than others to fashion the school-based policies and practices which
influence their daily encounters with pupils. To a large degree, pupils
inhabit a school edifice created by others.

We began our work on student disaffection by trying to identify the projects and approaches which appeared to be the most promising in tackling the problems faced by young people on the margins. Throughout the course of the work we have been drawn back into issues related to teaching and learning.

A complex range of factors to do with teachers, classrooms and schools, pupils and parents, impinge on the learning process. Undoubtedly, flexible and holistic solutions that address young people's long-term sense of the connections between learning and their prospects for the future are needed to deal with disaffection, truancy and exclusion. However, the needs, problems and backgrounds of disengaged young people are complex and diverse. The challenges which many of them face can change from day to day, as well as from year to year. For many disengaged students, schooling is only one small part of their worries and lives. Typically, they have a limited realization of the long-term impact and damage that being disengaged from schooling can have upon their future.

Whilst all this is true, what has also emerged strongly from our study is a shared belief amongst many of those we interviewed – parents, pupils and teachers – about the causes of disaffection, and an eagerness for things to be different. Parents, teachers and pupils are united in their views about the ingredients which make up the blueprint for change (Chapter 7, Table 7.2).

Three ingredients are needed to make that blueprint a reality – and there are messages here for both policy-makers and practitioners. First, *time and resources*: issues such as time, training and development opportunities, additional staff cannot be ignored. There is no lack of awareness on the ground, for example, that multi-agency approaches are needed to meet the challenges which many disaffected young people face. Change requires time and staffing, as well as commitment. Time is needed not simply for responding and planning, but also for reflecting, sharing and assessing whether approaches are working. What has come through our study very strongly is that there is willingness and enthusiasm to adopt new ways of working but, as one headteacher concluded in response to our proposals, 'They are all important, but I find it difficult to implement them due to lack of time, increasing bureaucracy and the speed of change ...'.

The second ingredient is to do with the *organizational, pedagogical and curriculum changes* which are needed to create a different environment for teaching and learning. Decisions about what those changes are need to be based on sound evidence about which approaches will work most effectively, and in what contexts. If resources are to be used wisely, then effective evaluation of projects and initiatives becomes a fundamental issue, rather than a luxury or 'add on', and dissemination of good practices becomes the norm, not the exception. An equally important supportive element is building the professional capacity of the practitioners undertaking change. Effective organizations and individuals thrive and rely on information which challenges their thinking and updates their practices. Success rests on the knowledge, expertise and confidence of those working in schools and with young people.

The final ingredient is to do with *attitudes and approaches* and applies as equally to policy-makers as practitioners. Changing institutional practices and shifting individual attitudes are less likely to arise through policy direction than through raising awareness and creating incentives for change, such as the encouragement of schools and agencies to 'sign up' through a charter-mark type arrangement to common goals and objectives. There needs to be an attitudinal shift on the part of governments and a recognition of the ways in which teachers can help shape policy, rather than always be shaped by it. We know that for many children and young people, schooling is a fragmented process. Practitioners need to be given the opportunity to experiment with new and radical ways of organizing teaching and learning. Some of these may test the boundaries of the school day, or week, or even our concept of what a school looks like. Trust is needed to help bring about a shift in power relations between government and schools. A parallel attitudinal shift is also needed at the school level, and within classrooms.

In the current national educational policy climate, there is pressure to produce measurable outcomes, to formulate evidence-based policies and to demonstrate change. In this book we have tried to put forward a more localized view about the ways in which inclusive polices aimed at tackling disaffection can be achieved by those on the ground: schools, practitioners, and local agencies and services. In our view, involving teachers and pupils in shaping the decisions and rules which impact on their daily lives will help change attitudes, expectations and relationships. Ultimately, this is what will make a difference to the lives of disaffected young people, their parents and communities.

Chapter notes

Chapter 2

1 The evidence that raising national attainment in areas such as literacy or numeracy boosts economic performance has not gone unchallenged (Robinson, 1998).

2 Despite a strong plea from the Commission for Racial Equality, no specific targets were set to reduce ethnic-minority overrepresentation in exclusions, particularly for Afro-Caribbean boys who are six times more likely to be excluded than their white counterparts (Ouseley, 1998). The government also refused to identify councils that excluded high numbers of black children, making it impossible to gauge whether the situation was improving or not (*TES*, 2000).

3 Education Action Zones (EAZs) were part of the Labour government's search for innovative ways of tackling underachievement and were introduced by the 1997 Labour administration. Education Action Zones were made up of clusters of primary, secondary and special schools working in partnership with the local education authority, local parents, business and Training and Enterprise Councils, and in some instances health or employment action zones (Riley et al., 1998; Riley and Watling, 1999). By 2001, EAZs had ceased to be a political priority (*TES*, 2001).

4 In 1999 several other initiatives were also introduced, most notably 'Excellence in Cities', which was designed to raise achievement in inner city schools. In early 2000, the UK government signalled a further range of new developments, including city academies (which were intended

to expand the role of the private sector in state education), 'The Connexions Strategy' which focused on enabling young people to participate in appropriate learning by raising their aspirations (DfEE, 2000b), and 'Schools Plus' which focuses on the most cost-effective approaches to using schools as a location for other community services aimed at reducing school failure (DfEE, 2000c).

5 In June 2001, a Labour government was re-elected for a second term of office. 'New Government, same priority "Education, Education, Education"' was how the renamed Education Department – the Department for Education and Skills – described the new policy agenda in its magazine for the teaching force, *Teachers*. New elements on the political agenda appear to be increased specialization of secondary schools and an expanding role for the private sector.

6 Our separate study on the 'Role and Effectiveness of the LEA' revealed some critical issues about practices and approaches to inclusion and suggested a discordance between the ways in which the national inclusion and achievement agendas play out at a local level (Riley, Docking and Rowles, 1998a, 1998b, 1999 and 2000).

7 A survey of primary and secondary school teachers in England conducted in March 2000 found that 52 per cent believed that their job as a teacher has become even more difficult over the past two years (*Guardian*, 2000).

8 Whilst much is known about the extent of exclusion and its long-term impact, our review revealed a long-standing tradition of viewing exclusion and disaffection as 'problems' of the individual student, rather than as a consequence of pedagogy, schooling or educational policy (Rustique-Forrester, 1999). Over the past decade explanations about exclusion have shifted from the student- and teacher-blaming accounts of the 1960s, 1970s and 1980s, to a more complex conceptualization of exclusion (which locates it within a wider set of school, social and policy-related factors). However, the tendency remains to emphasize students' background characteristics rather than issues of policy and pedagogy (ibid.). Policy proposals for reducing exclusions are still typically dependent on deficit models and strategies which rely on external social intervention, or which favour alternative, non-mainstream educational provision over policies which encourage changes in schools' and teachers' practices. The student voice, or the

teacher voice, are rarely heard – or if heard, rarely acted upon.

9 During the course of our preliminary work for this project, a number of other issues of particular significance emerged. These included the quality of teacher training; the nature and content of the professional development offered to teachers; the nature of the pressures on schools and teachers; the reasons for what appeared to be relatively high levels of teacher dissatisfaction; the allocation of individualized time for students and teachers to work together; and the structure of the school day and the school timetable. We have been able to explore many of these issues during the course of our work.

Chapter 3

1 Our separate study on the 'Role and Effectiveness of the LEA', in which Lancashire participated, revealed some critical issues about practices and approaches to inclusion (Riley et al., 1998a; 1998b; 2000).

2 Our working arrangements with our Lancashire partners have been extensive, wide-ranging, and professionally challenging and rewarding. The Chief Education Officer was directly involved in helping design the project framework and the Head of Strategic Planning, supported by his team, took a significant lead in working with us, by reviewing objectives and offering key insights and reflections. Staff within the Educational Welfare and Youth Services also played a critical role.

3 Given the nature and complexity of the information that we wished to obtain, we decided that interview methods and focus groups would be more appropriate than survey questionnaires.

4 Following the seminar, we presented our analysis to research and prac-titioner colleagues at a range of seminars and research conferences. On the basis of the feedback that we received from these seminars, an interim report was drafted in July 1999. This report was submitted to Lancashire County Council and to schools and agencies throughout Lancashire, and was used to promote further discussions and reflections.

5 We recognize that there are other important groups who have an important role, such as governors and support staff. We hope to be able to bring these groups into future work which we have planned in the area of student disaffection.

6 Whilst our sample of formal interviews should not be viewed as a sta-

tistically representative one, we are confident that it has provided us with a cross-section of views of different groups and different geographical areas.

Chapter 4

1 Lancashire already had some experience of setting up pupil panels. In 1998 six truancy panels (containing some 90 secondary school students from Lancashire, London and Central Scotland) were set up.
2 See note 1 above.
3 The importance of pupil – teacher interactions cannot be underestimated and has been the focus of research elsewhere. For example, Jean Ruddock and colleagues (Ruddock et al., 1996) have argued that positive conditions for learning are dependent on a number of variables including teachers showing respect and exercising fairness towards pupils, and pupils being given intellectual stimulation and a degree of autonomy.

Chapter 5

1 The Plowden Report (1967) has been seen variously as the harbinger of creative primary practice, or as opening the floodgates to permissiveness (Riley, 1998a).
2 For a discussion of these issues see Riley (1998a, ch. 9), or Vincent and Tomlinson (1997) who have argued that prevailing definitions of parental partnerships marginalize parents, particularly working-class ones.
3 These findings resemble those of earlier research, as discussed in Docking (1990, pp. 71–9).

Chapter 6

1 We held three teacher panels of 20 teachers in total and two head-teacher panels of 12 in total. Those interviewed were from different regions in Lancashire, and from schools which drew their intakes from

areas of both high and low social deprivation. Seven of the headteachers were from secondary schools and five from primary. The teacher panel members fell into a number of categories: those responsible for pupil behaviour or well being (e.g. Heads of Year); those responsible for pupils with special needs (special needs co-ordinators [SENCOs], learning support staff); those involved in specific school-based initiatives aimed at raising achievement (e.g. co-ordinators for the Single Regeneration Budget [SRB] project on raising pupils' achievement).

Chapter 8

1 See for example, Birmingham City Council (2000).
1 Adapted from Stockwell Park Secondary School (2000).
2 Rustique-Forrester (1999).
3 For example, see McLaughlin and Talbert (1993); National Commission on Teaching and America's Future (1996); Rayner, 1998.

Chapter 9

1 See, for example, Cooper (1993) and Parsons (1999).
2 For a broader discussion about the most effective ways of approaching the change process see Riley (2000).

References

Association of Teachers and Lecturers/Institute for Public Policy Research (ATL) (2000). *Teachers and Parents: A Survey of Teachers' Views* (ATL, 7 Northumberland, London WC2N 5DA).

Bengt-Andersson, E. (1997). 'Young adults look back on their situation in senior high school', paper to the European Conference on Educational Research, Frankfurt, September.

Birmingham City Council (2000). *Strategic Choices for Inclusion*, 8 February.

Brontë, C. (1980). *Jane Eyre*, Oxford: Oxford University Press.

Castle, F. and Parsons, C. (1997). 'Disruptive behaviour and exclusions from school: redefining and responding to the problem', *Emotional and Behavioural Difficulties*, vol. 2 no. 3, Winter, pp. 4–11.

Cooper, P. (1993). *Effective Schools for Disaffected Students: Integration and Segregation*, London: Routledge.

Cooper, P., Smith, C. and Upton, G. (1993). *Emotional and Behavioural Difficulties: Theory to Practice*, London: Routledge.

Department for Education and Employment (DfEE) (1999). *Statistical Release*, 11/99, London: DfEE.

Department for Education and Employment (DfEE) (2000a). *Statistics of Education: Pupil Absence and Truancy from Schools in England, 1998/99*, London: Stationery Office.

Department for Education and Employment (DfEE) (2000b). *Connexions*, London: DfEE.

Department for Education and Employment (DfEE) (2000c). *Schools Plus: Building Learning Communities*, report from the Policy Action Team 11,

London: DfEE (March).

Docking, J. (1987). *Control and Discipline in Schools: Perspectives and Approaches*, London: Harper and Row.

Docking, J. (1990). *Primary Schools and Parents: Rights, Responsibilities and Relationships*, London: Hodder and Stoughton.

Docking, J. (1996). *National School Policy: Major Issues in Educational Policy for Schools in England and Wales, 1979 Onwards*, London: David Fulton.

Guardian (2000). Guardian Education, 7 March, p. v.

House of Commons (1998) *Disaffected Children, Fifth Report, Volume I, Report and Proceedings of the Committee*, Education and Employment Committee, April, London: Stationery Office.

Hoyle, D. (1998). 'Constructions of pupil absence in the British educational system', *Child and Family Social Work*, vol. 3, pp. 1–13.

Kozol, J. (1996). *Amazing Grace*, New York: Harper Perennial.

Lindblad, S. (1997). 'Notes on youth culture and the micro-politics of schooling', Paper to the European Conference on Educational Research, Frankfurt, September.

Lovey, J., Docking, J. and Evans, R. (1993). *Exclusion from School: Provision for Disaffection at Key Stage 4*, London: David Fulton.

Lovey, J. (2000). 'Disengagement, exclusion and truancy', in J. Docking, (ed.) *New Labour's Policies for Schools: Raising the Standard?* London: David Fulton.

MacBeath, J., Moos, L. and Riley, K.A. (1996). 'Leadership in a changing world', in K. Leithwood., K. Chapman., C. Corson., P. Hallinger and A. Hart (eds) *International Handbook for Educational Leadership and Administration*, Netherlands: Kluwer Academic, pp. 223–50.

McEwan, A. and Thompson, W. (1997). 'After the national curriculum: teacher stress and morale', *Research in Education*, no. 57, pp. 57–66.

McLaughlin, M. and Talbert, J. (1993). *Contexts That Matter for Teaching and Learning*, Stanford, CA: Center for Research on the Context of Secondary School Teaching, Stanford University.

National Commission on Teaching and America's Future (1996). *What Matters Most: Teaching for America's Future*, New York: Columbia University.

Organization for Economic Co-operation and Development (OECD) (1995). *Educational Research and Development: Trends Issues and*

Challenges, Paris: Centre for Educational Research and Development, Organization for Economic Co-operation and Development.

Organization for Economic Co-operation and Development (OECD) (1996a). *Successful Services for our Children at Risk*, Paris: Organization for Economic Co-operation and Development.

Organization for Economic Co-operation and Development (OECD) (1996b). *Education at a Glance*, Paris: Organization for Economic Co-operation and Development.

Organization for Economic Co-operation and Development (OECD) (1996c). *Making Lifelong Learning a Reality for All*, Paris: Organization for Economic Co-operation and Development.

Organization for Economic Co-operation and Development (OECD) (1997). *Combating Failure at School*, Paris: Organization for Economic Co-operation and Development.

Osler, A. and Hill , J. (1998). 'Exclusion from school and racial equality: an examination of government proposal in the light of recent research evidence', *Cambridge Journal of Education*, vol. 28, no. 1, p. 33–59.

Ouseley, H. (1998). 'Stop being colour blind on exclusions', *Times Educational Supplement*, May 22, p. 14.

Parsons, C. (1999). *Education, Exclusion, and Citizenship*, London: Routledge.

Pearce, N. and Hillman, J. (1998). *Wasted Youth: Raising Achievement and Tackling Social Exclusion*, London: Institute for Public Policy Research.

The Plowden Report (1997). *Children and Their Primary Schools*, London: HMSO.

Rayner, S (1998). 'Educating pupils with emotional and behavioural difficulties: pedagogy is the key!' *Emotional and Behavioural Difficulties*, vol. 3, no. 2, pp. 39–47.

Riley, K.A. (1998a). *Whose School is it Anyway?* London: Falmer Press.

Riley, K.A. (1998b). *International Issues in Education: Trends and Challenges*, London: Local Government Management Board.

Riley, K.A. (2000). 'Leadership Learning and Systemic Reform', *Journal of Education Change*, vol 1, no. 1, pp. 29–55, Netherlands: Kluwer Academic.

Riley. K.A., (2001). *Promoting Good Teaching and Learning*, Effective Schools and Teachers, World Bank: Washington, DC.

Riley. K.A., Docking, J. and Rowles, D. (1998a). 'LEAs on probation – Will they Meet the Grade?' *Education Review*, vol. 12, no. 1, pp. 30–35.

Riley. K.A., Docking, J. and Rowles, D. (1998b). 'The changing role and effectiveness of the local education authority', *Education Journal*, April, pp. 6–7.

Riley. K.A., Docking, J. and Rowles, D. (1999). 'Can local education authorities make a difference?' (The perceptions of users and providers), *Education Management and Administration*, vol. 27, no. 1, pp. 29–44.

Riley. K.A., Docking, J. and Rowles, D. (2000). 'Caught between: local education authorities, making a difference through their leadership?', in K.A. Riley and K.S. Louis (eds) *Leadership for Change and School Reform*, London: Falmer Press.

Riley. K.A., Docking, J., Rustique-Forrester, E. and Rowles, D. (2001). 'Burntwood Secondary Girls School' in M. Madden (ed.) *Success Against the Odds – Five Years On: Revisiting Effective Schools in Disadvantaged Areas*, Routledge/Falmer Press, pp. 152–83.

Riley, K.A. and Louis, K.S.L. (2000). *Leadership for Change and School Reform, International Perspectives on Leadership*, London: Falmer Press.

Riley. K.A. and Skelcher, C. (1998). *Local Education Authorities: A Schools' Service, or a Local Authority Service?* London: Local Government Management Board.

Riley, K.A., Watling, R., Rowles, D. and Hopkins, D. (1998). *Some Lessons Learned from the First Wave of Education Action Zones*, London: The Education Network, October.

Riley, K.A.. and Watling, R. (1999). 'Education Action Zones: an initiative in the making', *Public Money and Management*, vol. 19, no. 3, pp. 51–8.

Robinson, P. (1998). 'The tyranny of league tables: international comparisons of educational attainment and economic performance', paper for the Seminar on Comparative Research on Pupil Achievement, University of Bristol, March.

Ruddock, J., Chalpain, R. and Wallace, G. (eds) (1996). *School Improvement: What Can Pupils Tell Us?* London: David Fulton.

Rustique-Forrester, E. (1999). 'The growing disaffection and exclusion of young people: a literature review', paper presented at the Annual Conference, British Educational Research Association, University of Sussex, London: Centre for Educational Management, University of Surrey Roehampton.

Sarason, S. (1990). *The Predictable Failure of Educational Reform*, San Francisco and Oxford: Jossey-Bass.

School Standards and Framework Act (1998). London: HMSO.

Social Exclusion Unit (SEU) (1998). *Truancy and School Exclusion*, Report by the Social Exclusion Unit, May, Cm 395, London: HMSO.

Stockwell Park Secondary School (2000). *Behaviour Policy and Procedures Guide*, London: Stockwell Secondary School.

Times Educational Supplement (*TES*) (2000). 9 June, p.3.

Times Educational Supplement (*TES*) (2001). 5 January, p. 1.

UNISON and the National Association of Social Workers in Education (1998). *Truancy and Social Exclusion, Submission to the Social Exclusion Unit*, March, London: UNISON.

Vincent, C and Tomlinson, S. (1997). 'Home school relationships,' *British Educational Research Journal*, vol. 23, no. 3, pp. 361–77.

Whitty, G., Power, S. and Halpin, D. (1998). *Devolution and Choice in Education: The School, the State, and the Market*, Buckingham: Open University Press.

Index

Added to a page number {t} denotes a table and {f} denotes a figure. Page numbers in italic refer to boxes.